The
THEOLOGY
of the BODY
in JOHN PAUL II

What It Means, Why It Matters

RICHARD M. HOGAN

The Word Among Us Press
9639 Doctor Perry Road
Ijamsville, Maryland 21754
www.wordamongus.org
13 12 11 10 09   2 3 4 5 6

ISBN: 978-1-59325-086-7

The original Catechesis extracts of Pope John Paul II and then Cardinal Karol Wojtyla, copyright © Libreria Editrice Vaticana, 00120 Vatican City State. The texts may be traced on the Vatican website: www.vatican.va. Used by permission.

Scripture texts used in this work are taken from the Revised Standard Version Bible: Catholic Edition, © 1965 and 1966 by the Division of Christian Education of the National Council of the Churches of Christ in the USA. All rights reserved. Used with permission.

Cover design by Laura Steur-Alvarez

Nihil obstat: Rev. Paul F. deLadurantaye
    Censor deputatus

Imprimatur: Rev. Frank J. Ready, Vicar General
    October 16, 2006

The *nihil obstat* and *imprimatur* are official declarations that a book or pamphlet is free of doctrinal or moral error. No implication is contained therein that those who have granted the *nihil obstat* and *imprimatur* agree with the contents, opinions, or statements expressed.

Library of Congress Cataloging-in-Publication Data
Hogan, Richard M.
  The theology of the body in John Paul II : what it means, why it matters / Richard M. Hogan.
    p. cm.
  Includes bibliographical references.
  ISBN-13: 978-1-59325-086-7 (alk. paper)
  1. John Paul II, Pope, 1920-2005. Theology of the body. 2. Body, Human--Religious aspects--Catholic Church. 3. Catholic Church--Doctrines. I. Title.
  BX1795.B63H645 2006
  233'.5--dc22
                          2006030347

Contents

Foreword

I first met Fr. Richard Hogan some years ago when he visited the Diocese of Cheyenne, where at the time I was coadjutor bishop. He and I traveled the Diocese of Cheyenne for a week making presentations to deanery gatherings of the Wyoming Council of Catholic Women. As Wyoming is a large state and the Diocese of Cheyenne covers the entire state, we spent many hours in the van together. Since that week, I and others on the diocesan staff have invited Fr. Hogan to return to discuss the teaching of Pope John Paul II and, in particular, his theology of the body addresses, in a variety of venues in the diocese.

As Fr. Hogan argues in this volume, the teaching of Pope John Paul II will remain with the church for centuries. John Paul "the Great" certainly developed a new way of explaining the gospel by uniting the truths of revelation with the modern philosophical movement called phenomenology. One of the results of this marriage of phenomenology and the truths of the faith is John Paul II's theology of the body.

Certainly, since the 1960s, there has been what some have identified as culture wars in the Western world. Does the heritage of European thought and civilization, which was built on the idea that human beings are created in the image and likeness of God, still hold? Or, do we embrace the competing idea that human beings are merely an accident of evolution and biology who have no more claim to dignity and value than, say, dolphins or whales? At the heart of the cultural problem today is: Who is man? Who is the human being in his or her body/soul unity? If the answer is that a human being is simply a fluke of nature, then perhaps the ideas of the sexual revolution should be embraced. On the other hand, if the answer is that a human being is truly a transcendent being whose body is the expression of his or her person, and even the expression of the divine, then the received tradition would still hold and it should inform and form our culture!

Who is man? This, I suggest, is the key question and the one which our late pope spent a lifetime answering. Certainly, it was the key question of his papacy. John Paul's theology of the body addresses form a partial answer to this key question. Fr. Hogan has given us in this volume some new insights into John Paul II's thought and certainly provided us with some profound interpretations of the material. One of the strengths of this work is Father's long study of the pope's theology of the body addresses (twenty-five years or more) and his synthetic knowledge of the other works of Pope John Paul II.

Most Reverend David Ricken, DD, JCL
Bishop of Cheyenne, Wyoming

Introduction

In his book *Witness to Hope*, biographer George Weigel suggests that Pope John Paul II's theology of the body is a "theological time bomb set to go off, with dramatic consequences, sometime in the third millennium of the Church."[1] Many in the church would agree that the bomb has already exploded. Today the theology of the body is the subject of a host of books, study guides, conferences, and parish seminars. This growing interest in the pope's work comes at a time when many in secular society have grown tired of the ways in which sexuality and the human body are either demeaned, on the one hand, or idolized, on the other.

The subtitle of this book asks why the theology of the body matters. The answer is that John Paul II's work breaks new ground in presenting the timeless truths of the faith in a way that people of the twenty-first century can understand. It is my contention, developed in this book, that this new synthesis of the faith will speak to modern-day people in a way that older presentations of the faith can no longer do.

The theology of the body is a series of addresses given by Pope John Paul II at his Wednesday papal audiences in Rome from September 1979 to November 1984. (There were some rather lengthy interruptions in this series, such as during the Holy Year of the Redemption in 1983.) The Wednesday papal audiences are an opportunity for visitors and pilgrims to Rome to see and hear the pope. Previous popes of the second half of the twentieth century have also given addresses at these audiences. However, John Paul II's predecessors have not tried to give a series of addresses devoted to one theme in successive audiences. Rather, each address stood on its own and treated a subject appropriate to that particular Wednesday. For example, on a saint's feast day, Pope Paul VI might have spoken about that particular saint; or during the Easter season, Pope John XXIII might have addressed the joys of Easter and the promise of the resurrection of the body implicit in Christ's resurrection.

John Paul II decided to use the Wednesday audiences to give a series of addresses devoted to one central theme. The topic of the first of these series was the theology of the body. A series, given once a week to totally different audiences over several years, is not the easiest task to attempt. Each address needs to stand on its own and make sense to the particular audience who hears it. Still, it must fit into the series and be part of a much larger effort to address the central theme. In order to establish a context for the current talk, the pope begins each address by summarizing the main points of the previous talk.

The theology of the body series comprises a 129 individual addresses. These are divided into six different cycles. Each chapter of this book is devoted to one cycle, in which I provide a commentary on the pope's major points. In the first cycle (addresses 1–23), John Paul discusses Christ's answer to the Pharisees when they asked him about whether a man can divorce his wife.[2] The second cycle (addresses 24–63) is a reflection on Christ's remarks in the Sermon on the Mount about adultery, "You have heard that it was said, 'You shall not commit adultery.' But I say to you, every one who looks at a woman lustfully has already committed adultery with her in his heart."[3] The third cycle (addresses 64–72) discusses the resurrection of the body through an analysis of Christ's answer to the Sadducees when they questioned him about the resurrection of the body.[4] As the subtitle promises, my aim in writing this book was also to explain what the pope means in his talks. While my commentary is not meant to be an exhaustive approach, it will provide the reader with the general thread of the pope's thought and reasoning.

The concept that the human body is the expression of the human person is one of the guiding principles of the entire theology of the body series. It is also the basis for the first three cycles of the series, which focus on the three ways that the human body expresses the person: in paradise before sin (first cycle); in the world today after sin and before the resurrection of the body (second cycle); and in heaven after the second coming, when our bodies will be resurrected (third cycle). In answering the Pharisees' question about divorce, Christ refers to "the beginning." This reference was to the first words of Genesis, and so John Paul begins an analysis of the way the human body expresses the persons of Adam and Eve before sin (first cycle). Then, citing Christ's words about "looking lustfully," John Paul sees a reference to sin and so he begins an analysis of the human person in his or her body/person structure after sin and before the resurrection of the body (second cycle). Quoting Christ's words about the resurrected body in Christ's answer to the Sadducees, John Paul examines the way the human body expresses the person in heaven after the resurrection of the body (third cycle).

In the theology of the body series, John Paul establishes the *structure* of the individual human person in the body/person unity in the first three cycles, and only after this structure is unfolded does he move on to examine what such a person ought to do. Before one can understand what something does, it is essential to understand what it is! As Aristotle and St. Thomas Aquinas both taught (John Paul is a follower of both Aristotle and Aquinas), action follows on being. One looks at what something does only after studying what that object is. With human persons, it is necessary to study the mystery of person-hood in the body/person structure before examining how we should act—that we should love as God loves.

The last three cycles apply the points previously discussed to vocations in this life. The fourth cycle (addresses 73–86) discusses the conclusions of the first three cycles in relation to celibacy and virginity for the sake of the king-dom. The fifth cycle (adddresses 87–113), a particularly vital one, is an exten-sive analysis of St. Paul's teaching on marriage in his Letter to the Ephesians (Ephesians 5:21-32) in light of the conclusions previously reached in the first three cycles of the theology of the body. The sixth cycle (addresses 114–129) applies the conclusions of the first three cycles to the teaching of the church regarding procreation.

In addition to the emphasis on the vital principle that the human body is the expression of the human person, there are a number of other insights that are essential to the interpretation of John Paul's teaching offered here:

- The theology of the body is, in part, the result of the application of a rela-tively new philosophical movement, known as phenomenology, to the truths of the faith. This philosophy gives the papal teaching its new "tone" and "tenor" as distinguished from the traditions found in St. Augustine (who used the philosophy of Plato) and St. Thomas (who used the philosophy of Aristotle).

- The term "meaning" in the theology of the body series, (such as when it is used in "the nuptial meaning of the body"),[5] denotes the knowledge a human person gains from reflection on an experience she or he has had. For example, the "nuptial meaning of the body" refers to the understanding that Adam and Eve had from their experiences of their own masculinity and femininity. The "meaning" is that they realized they were to be a self-gift to one another.

• The term "spousal love,"[6] used in the fifth cycle of the theology of the body, is applied to Christ. It is argued in the section of this work on the fifth cycle that "spousal love" means a love expressed in and through a human body. Christ's love was "spousal" because his love was made visible through his human body.

• The great comparison that St. Paul makes in Ephesians 5 between the union of Christ and the church, on the one hand, and the union of husband and wife, on the other, is usually understood as an image illuminating the union of Christ and the church. While that interpretation is certainly accepted in the theology of the body series, John Paul clearly emphasizes that the comparison also *must* be read as explaining marriage. In other words, the profound union of Christ and the church must be a model for the union of husband and wife.

• Also in reference to Ephesians 5, it is clear that the image of the church as the mystical body/person of Christ, taught by St. Paul[7], must always be held in conjunction with the church as the bride of Christ. These two images of the church are both true, and both must be interpreted in light of one another. The image of the church as the mystical body/person of Christ underlines the oneness of Christ and the church, which in no way can be contradicted by the bridal image. The church as bride and Christ as groom become one to the point that they form one body/person, a greater oneness than any human marriage could ever achieve.

It should also be noted that all Scripture quotations are taken from the Revised Standard Version unless the Scripture passage is quoted within a text taken from one of the theology of the body addresses. In this case, the quotation as given in the papal text is followed. In addition, all quotations from the theology of the body addresses are from the English edition of *L'Osservatore Romano,* which is also the source for *The Theology of the Body: Human Love in the Divine Plan* (Pauline Books and Media, 1997). These quotations are cited with the abbreviation TB (for "theology of the body"), along with the number of the address. (A list of the addresses including their number, title, and date is provided on p. 215 of this book.) For your convenience, the paragraph/section number in *L'Osservatore Romano* (in parentheses) and the page number in the Pauline edition are both given.

Working through John Paul's theology of the body is not easy, but it is rewarding. As readers come to a deeper understanding of the pope's message, I pray that they will grow in appreciation for the gift of their bodies, for life itself, and for a pope who reveals so brilliantly the beauty of our faith. He certainly deserves the title of John Paul the Great, as was proclaimed by the crowd at his funeral!

I had the privilege of meeting Pope John Paul II a few times. On one occasion in June, 1985, I was privileged to hand the pope a copy of *Covenant of Love,* a book I had written together with the Rev. John M. LeVoir. While shaking hands with John Paul, I thanked him for his theology of the body addresses. He seemed surprised, probably because he was not accustomed to receiving such comments at papal audiences. In any case, my first debt of thanks is to Pope John Paul II.

I am also deeply indebted to all those people who have attended lectures and talks I have given on the theology of John Paul II. Comments and questions of many, many people over more than twenty years have stimulated my thoughts and led me to further consideration of important points.

I owe a very special debt of thanks to Bob and Gerri Laird of the Arlington (Virginia) diocese. I have been able to assist them in renewing the engaged program in their diocese and have also been invited numerous times to make presentations at the engaged conferences. The remarks and questions of engaged couples have been particularly helpful in developing portions of this volume. I also want to thank both of them for inviting me to record my thoughts and ideas in audio and audiovisual formats. Of course, none of this work could have been carried out without the support of the priests and particularly the bishop of the Arlington diocese. I owe a debt of gratitude to all of them and in particular to Bishop Paul Loverde.

I also want to thank Archbishop Harry Flynn of the Archdiocese of St. Paul and Minneapolis. Without his kind permission to work with Natural Family Planning Outreach traveling the country giving presentations regarding Natural Family Planning and the theology of the body addresses, I doubt that this book would have been written.

I am grateful to all those who have organized my visits to parishes, conventions, meetings, and other gatherings where I have made presentations.

A great debt of thanks goes to the founder and executive director of Natural Family Planning Outreach, the Rev. Daniel McCaffrey. He has given me the time and the support necessary to undertake the task of researching and writing this book. I am indeed privileged to be working with him. Also, John Fitzgerald of Fitzgerald and Fitzgerald in Yonkers, New York, must be mentioned. He has been conspicuously generous in supporting Natural Family Planning Outreach and me personally through the St. Augustine Foundation, which he established. This foundation is competently run by Dorothy Dugandzic, who I also wish to thank.

To my friends and family who have sustained me while working on this project, I am profoundly grateful. I wish to mention to my mother, Jeanne C. Hogan, and my very close friends, Nancy and Jerry Rankin, and their immediate and extended family. Their support and prayers have been invaluable.

Finally, a word of thanks must be given to my editor, Patty Mitchell, and her co-workers at The Word Among Us Press. I have been honored to work with Patty and her team.

Rev. Richard M. Hogan
September 29, 2006
Feast of Sts. Michael, Gabriel, and Raphael, Archangels

1. See George Weigel, *Witness to Hope: The Biography of Pope John Paul II* (New York: Cliff Street Books, 1999), p. 343.

2. See Matthew 19:3-9 and Mark 10:2-9.

3. See Matthew 5:27-28.

4. See Matthew 22:23-33.

5. See TB, no. 14.

6. See TB, nos. 91, 93.

7. See Ephesians 5:23. See also Richard M. Hogan and John M. LeVoir, *Covenant of Love*, 2nd ed. (San Francisco: Ignatius Press, 1992), pp. 145–52. See also Richard M. Hogan and John M. LeVoir, *Faith for Today*, 2nd ed. (Boston: St. Paul Books and Media, 1995), pp. 152–58.

Prologue

The John Paul II Revolution

A. A New Approach to Theology

1. St. Augustine, St. Thomas, and Pope John Paul II

From the very first words of the theology of the body, one realizes that John Paul II's approach to theology differs from those taken by the great representatives of the Catholic theological tradition, St. Augustine and St. Thomas Aquinas. St. Augustine represents the first attempt in the West to develop a unified presentation of the faith through the use of a particular philosophical system. In adapting Plato's philosophical thought to the data of revelation, Augustine formulated a synthesis of the Catholic faith. The faith was taught in terms of this synthesis from Augustine's death in 430 until the thirteenth century.

By the thirteenth century, culture and modes of thought had changed. Arabic translations of the works of Aristotle, translated into Latin in Spain, had become available to scholars in Europe. Later, direct translations from the original Greek texts to Latin became available through the Crusader states established in the Holy Land. Not only did these new translations provide more accurate texts of works already known, but works previously unknown to medieval Europeans became available. Aristotle's works changed the academic world of the thirteenth century, as did other factors as well. No longer did the Augustinian system convey the faith in terms easily understood. It was necessary to develop a new synthesis, a new way of conveying the faith. St. Thomas did for this period what St. Augustine had done for his, except that instead of Plato, St. Thomas used Aristotle. The resulting theological synthesis became the second mode of conveying the faith in the West.

While rooted in both the Augustinian and Thomistic traditions, John Paul's theology of the body has a startling and unexpected new twist. Together with his other works, it represents a new synthesis, a new way of conveying the faith to the modern world. This new approach is necessary because most people in the twentieth and twenty-first centuries do not think and act in the categories of either St. Augustine or St. Thomas.

2. The Twenty-First Century in Contrast with the Medieval World

Both St. Augustine and St. Thomas Aquinas lived and taught in cultures that might be described as objective, deductive, and principled. The modern world is primarily subjective, inductive, and experiential. To call something "objective" means that it is real, that is, that it is true regardless of whether or not anyone knows it to be true. For example, if a blind man is in a forest, the trees are still there. The objective existence of the trees does not depend on whether or not the man perceives them. Objective reality exists independent of anyone's perception. The subjective view of reality claims that only what I perceive to be real is actually real. Generally, the subjective view of reality is not applied to trees and other physical objects. However, it is applied to nonphysical realities, for example, God and moral principles. The subjective view of reality is captured by the phrase "That may be true for you, but not for me!" In other words, what is true depends on what I believe or accept, what I perceive. In the medieval world, such a claim would have been utter nonsense. In fact, to most medieval academics, the truths of the faith, both dogmatic and moral, were more real than physical objects. The medieval world was objective. We are subjective.

The medieval world was also deductive, which is consistent with its objective view of the world. Knowledge was derived from principles by the process of deduction, often illustrated in syllogisms. One started with what was called the major premise—a given that was already accepted, for instance, that God is a pure spirit—and added what was called the minor premise, for instance, that a pure spirit does not have a body. One could then draw a conclusion, in this case, that God does not have a body. In our era, most people would agree that truth is discovered by experiments, by our own experience, and by counting heads—whatever the majority believes. These methods of reaching truth or knowledge are inductive—a method that involves a different process from the deductive method.

The third difference between a principled and an experiential world-view is implied by the other two. The medieval culture was based on widely accepted truths from which conclusions were drawn; that is, on principles. The modern world generally derives knowledge from personal experiences and experimentation.

3. The Need for a New Synthesis

Since most in our era think subjectively, inductively, and experientially, they are ill prepared to hear, even less to understand, the truths and practices of the faith taught in a structure and outline that is objective, deductive, and principled. Even the vocabulary and language used in the Augustinian and Thomistic syntheses are foreign to the modern ear. If the revelation of Christ is to be grasped and understood today, it needs to be presented to people in their own language and in their own modes of thought. Thus, it needs to have a subjective, inductive, and experiential garb, and it needs to use words that are part of the common coinage of modern culture. The challenge is to take the jewels of the faith—the revelation of Christ—and present them in a new way with a new philosophical system *without changing their content*. We need to have another genius, another St. Augustine or St. Thomas, who can do for our era what those saints did for theirs. In this sense, John Paul II was indeed another Augustine, another Thomas. He placed the jewels of the faith into a new setting; he gave them a mode and a garb that makes them understandable to our age.

The church needs to convey the content of revelation in a way that is understandable to people of every generation. That is what St. Thomas did for the thirteenth century. Yet there were those who insisted on continuing to use the traditional explanations; that is, the synthesis of St. Augustine. John Paul II has presented a new synthesis for our generation. This raises the question whether, if one understands the Thomistic or Augustinian synthesis, there is any harm in using them. Of course not. They need to be taught to every generation of theologians. However, as a way of conveying the faith to the people of the twenty-first century, it seems that the new John Paul II synthesis is more effective.

Many will insist that John Paul II is a Thomist. Of course, he is! St. Thomas was an Augustinian! Each new synthesis builds on the previous ones. There is no question that John Paul II is a Thomist. But there is also no question that he built a new theological synthesis, which will be one of the building blocks of the church in the twenty-first century and beyond. The Augustinian synthesis was the way the church thought about revelation for about eight hundred years. St. Thomas' synthesis was in place for more than seven hundred years. If the pattern holds, John Paul II's synthesis will be with us for centuries.

B. Phenomenology: John Paul II's Personalistic Philosophy

1. An Analogy

Although John Paul II takes a new approach to the faith, he doesn't change the faith at all. To understand what he has done, consider this analogy. The content of the faith, the revelation of Christ, can be compared to a large diamond resting on a pedestal in the middle of a room in a museum. The diamond can be viewed from any point outside the circular guardrail that surrounds it. Similarly, the context of the faith can be viewed from a variety of philosophical viewpoints. We might say that St. Augustine looked at the diamond from one vantage point, using Platonic philosophy. St. Thomas moved to another point on the circumference, using Aristotle. John Paul has adopted a third point of observation, using a philosophical movement called phenomenology. Actually, since John Paul was a Thomist and an Augustinian, and Thomas himself was an Augustinian, we would have to make the analogy a little more complicated. Perhaps we should think of Thomas standing on the shoulders of Augustine, and John Paul standing on the shoulders of Thomas. Rather than standing around the diamond, the three men are at different heights in front of it!

In any case, Augustine, Thomas, and John Paul are looking at the very same diamond. Yet each onlooker can point out a particular features to another. All the observers see the same things, but they describe them differently because of the different philosophical systems they use. Therefore, it is possible to translate the description of any feature of the diamond from Augustine to Thomas to John Paul II, or from John Paul II to Thomas and Augustine, and so on. It is always the same diamond that is described by each speaker.

Through phenomenology, John Paul has been able to present the content of Christ's revelation in a subjective, inductive, and experiential way without doing damage to its content. The new theological synthesis he has produced is usually called "personalism." The new twist in John Paul II's theology of the body is the application of this personalistic approach to the problems of sexuality, marriage, and family life.

2. A New Interpretation of All Revelation

In his *Witness to Hope*, George Weigel, quoting Cardinal Angelo Scola, writes that "virtually every thesis in theology—God, Christ, the Trinity, grace, the church, the sacraments—could be seen in a new light if theologians explored in depth the rich personalism implied in John Paul II's theology of the body."[1] This remark is absolutely true, for two reasons. First, the new synthesis of Pope John Paul II is clearly apparent in his theology of the body, and it can be studied and learned from these addresses. Once learned, it will be recognized in other writings of the pope. With the understanding thus gained, his initial work can be further developed. It should be noted that the founder of a new synthesis simply does the initial work, after which centuries are devoted to mining its riches. St. Augustine's synthesis, using Platonic philosophy, was studied and developed further over eight centuries. Similarly, St. Thomas' fusion of Aristotle's philosophy and the content of revelation was the subject of study and development that goes on even today. Certainly, if the new synthesis of John Paul II is studied in the theology of the body and then applied to other areas, "virtually every thesis in theology . . . could be seen in a new light."

Second, Weigel's remark is true because every area of revelation has an impact on other areas. How one understands the mystery of Christ, both his incarnation and redemption, will affect one's understanding of the church, of grace, of the sacraments, and the rest. How one understands the mystery of our creation in the image and likeness of God clearly affects one's concept of the second Person of the Trinity's becoming man. Revelation is a unified whole. It is Christ, and Christ cannot be subdivided. Since any new approach in one area will affect all others, of course John Paul II's new approach in the area of sexuality, marriage, and family life in the theology of the body will affect every thesis in theology, and "every thesis in theology. . . could be seen in a new light."

3. What Is Phenomenology?

The founder of phenomenology was a German philosopher named Edmund Husserl (1859–1938). Husserl, like all philosophers, was trying to investigate the mystery of human personhood. He did this by studying the individual's interior perception of the world. Each of us has experiences every day. These are experiences of reality outside ourselves—the world of nature, other people, manmade things, and so on. As persons, we not only have these experiences, but we also have an awareness of ourselves experiencing these things. Let us say that Joe attends a lecture. During the lecture, Joe experiences a reality outside of himself: the lecturer and what she says. In addition, however, Joe *knows* that he is having this experience. He is aware that he is experiencing the lecture. The power of self-awarenesss in each of us is called our consciousness. Husserl was interested in probing our consciousness, our self-awareness, of our experiences. While he focused on our experiences, however, Husserl insisted that they are experiences are of a reality outside ourselves.

In this way, Husserl linked the interior powers of the mind, will, and self-awareness, on the one side, with the real world, on the other. Thus he was able to overcome the division between the interior life of the mind and the real world that had entered philosophical thought through the French philosopher Descartes in the seventeenth century. Descartes' famous dictum, "I think, therefore I am," divorced reality (the exterior world) from the mind (the interior life of every person), because it grounded existence only in the interior, in thought.

Phenomenology studies human personhood *from the inside.* Since personhood is one of the most important concepts in Christianity, the phenomenological method provides a new way of studying and perceiving Christian revelation. St. Thomas, using Aristotle, studied personhood more or less from the outside, in an objective way. But "he did not adequately develop the subjective side of the life of the person."[2] Using the phenomenological method, John Paul is able to develop the subjective side of the person, while in no way compromising or altering the fundamental objective truths of revelation.

4. The Objective and Subjective Worlds Meet in the Human Person

It is precisely because the person is vital to revealed truth that there can be a synthesis of phenomenology and the faith. Phenomenology begins its investigation with the individual human person, specifically with our conscious experience of ourselves as acting agents. Phenomenology thus leads to the mystery of human personhood. Even though it is subjective, if phenomenology is used properly, it can lead to the objective truth about man revealed by God, that is, that human beings are made in God's image.[3] We have an awareness of our own acts—one of the most important marks of personhood—because we are like God, made in God's own image. This truth about the nature of human persons is revealed in the objective order, but through phenomenology it can be studied in a subjective way. The objective order of revelation is linked in this fashion with the subjective experience of each human person. It is no wonder that one of the hallmarks of John Paul II's pontificate was his repeated and insistent teaching on the dignity and value of each and every human person.

5. John Paul as Student of Philosophy

Karol Wojtyla first encountered phenomenology through Roman Ingarden, who was a professor in the philosophy department at the University of Cracow, where the future pope was earning his doctorate in philosophy. Ingarden had been one of Husserl's students. Through his studies, which focused on morality and ethics, Wojtyla saw that phenomenology was able to ground ethical norms in reality and not only in interior ideas.

Wojtyla wrote his doctoral dissertation on Max Scheler, who also had been a student of Husserl. Scheler attempted to come to knowledge of ethical norms through phenomenology. He argued that every human experience is connected with a value: we are either attracted to a given experience or repulsed by it. Each experience has a positive or negative "charge," that is, a positive or negative value. These values actually exist in the real world. They are concrete and objective but are known through subjective, individual experience. Rather than being commands that one is compelled to follow from the outside, ethical norms become part of one's own interior experience.

Wojtyla was critical of Scheler for failing to provide an objective order of values. Since values were known through the subjective experience of each person, persons could differ radically from one another in the values they held. Further, the relative importance of these values was determined by the intensity of the individual's response to each value. The value that elicited the most intense emotional response was, for that individual, the most important value. Therefore, even if two people had a similar set of values, their hierarchy of these values would differ. In Scheler's thought, there was no way to establish an objective order of morality.

Wojtyla was also critical of Scheler for another reason. Since we watch ourselves experience things through our consciousness, our self-awareness, every experience we have is contained within us in our consciousness. For example, if I constantly practice the piano and watch myself practicing, the experience of practicing the piano becomes stored within me in my consciousness. Since my consciousness is very much a part of me and is shaped and changed by my experiences, I constantly shape and reshape myself by the experiences I choose to have. If I choose repeatedly to practice the piano, I shape myself into someone who practices the piano. Phenomenologists, particularly Pope John Paul II, make this point by saying that "we become what we do." We become good or evil by doing good or evil acts. An ethical act not only has effects outside of ourselves; it also has an internal effect. Visiting a friend in the hospital not only benefits my friend, it also has an interior effect on me: I become a visitor of the sick. Scheler did not notice these internal, reflexive effects of ethical acts.

Despite Wojtyla's criticisms of Scheler's work, he saw that Scheler's use of phenomenology provided a powerful tool for the study of Christian ethics. If the Christian norms taught by revelation could be understood as interior norms, that is, if these norms could be perceived through experience, they would cease to have the character of external laws imposed on one from the outside. Further, one could speak about these values in a subjective way appropriate to the modern world.

C. Phenomenology and the Theology of the Body

The phenomenological method applied in theological reflection is at the heart of John Paul II's theology of the body. If the method is not clearly understood, then the principle points of theology of the body will be missed or, at least, misinterpreted. To use a favorite phrase of John Paul II, let us "reread" his theology of the body in light of his phenomenological method.

1. Scripture: Revelation of God through Human Experiences

The theology of the body series is in large part a study of the first three chapters of Genesis. The Scriptures contain the revelation of God. How is it possible to apply the phenomenological method, which studies human experiences, to revealed truths? This fundamental question, of course, is obvious when one examines the writings of John Paul II. God does not reveal himself to us from on high. He does not usually shout from the mountaintops at us. Rather, revelation occurs through the everyday experiences of life.

The comedian Bill Cosby indirectly made precisely this point with a routine that parodies the idea that God speaks to us from out of the blue. Cosby mimics both God and Noah. God begins by shouting at Noah from the heavens, "Hey, Noah!" Noah answers, "What do you want now?" God replies by asking Noah to build an ark. Noah asks God, "What's an ark?" God tells Noah, "An ark is a very big boat." Noah responds, "But, God, this is a desert!" God answers, "It won't be for long!" The exchange, paraphrased here, is comic not just because of Cosby's talent in performing it, but also because, for almost all religions, God is *not* just a voice from the sky. Rather, God comes to people and reveals himself. This is especially true for the Christian, who understands God through the incarnate Son!

God became man in order to relate to us in a completely human way. People met him and heard him. They had experiences of him and with him. These experiences, containing the truths of revelation, can be the subject of a phenomenological investigation. The meetings of people with Christ are experiential—and therefore can be studied phenomenologically—while containing the content of revelation.

2. Questions and Answers

When phenomenologists study human experiences, they are attempting to probe the mystery of personhood. For example, Scheler studied romantic love, because authentic love exchanged between a man and a woman is usually a life-changing event. Such an experience leads the person to ask questions such as "Who am I? Where am I going? Why am I here?" These questions are at the heart of the mystery of human personhood. Through the study of such experiences, phenomenologists are able to touch the heart of the mystery of human personhood. But phenomenology cannot answer such questions adequately. No philosophical method can, because at the heart of human personhood is the mystery that we were created in God's image and likeness for him. Only in God can human persons find the answers to the central questions about themselves. Therefore, only in revelation do we encounter the answers we need.

When phenomenology is applied to the experiences recorded in the

Scriptures, there is, so to speak, a double flow of data. There is the data that would come from any study of human experience that leads to the mystery of human personhood; in addition, there is the data of revelation, which answers the questions raised by the phenomenological study of human personhood.

3. Genesis 1–3: Two Accounts of Creation

In the first chapter of Genesis, the creation of human persons is revealed in an objective way. In the second and third chapters, we see the record of Adam and Eve's experiences of the event of creation and the fall. John Paul acknowledges that he wishes to look at the subjective, interior reality of the lives of our first parents, when he remarks that the second chapter of Genesis "presents the creation of man especially in its subjective aspect."[4]

In other words, the second and third chapters of Genesis are the record of Adam and Eve's consciousness of what happened to them. John Paul employs the phenomenological methods to study this record of Adam and Eve's consciousness of the events surrounding creation. But, since these texts are the inspired word of God, that is, revelation, they not only form the record of Adam and Eve's self-awareness of what they experienced but also answer the questions raised by such a philosophical investigation. Further, the theological truths about creation revealed in the first chapter of Genesis in an objective way act as a control on the theological conclusions reached through the experiment of applying phenomenology to the experiences recorded in the second and third chapters.

D. A Comprehensive New Presentation of the Gospel

The new synthesis of John Paul II encompasses the entire diamond—the whole content of Christ's revelation. The teachings of Christ can be outlined in seven general subject areas: God as one and triune, creation, Christ, church, sacraments, grace, and commandments. Under each of these is an immense amount of material, which in turn is divided into subcategories. For example, any complete discussion of the mystery of creation necessarily includes the creation of the angels, the creation of human persons, original sin, the effects of sin, and even the providence of God shown to the people of the Old Testament. John Paul II's new approach embraces all this. While there are a few subjects in revelation that John Paul did not address extensively, these can easily be studied according to the approach he took in his teaching on other topics. He has at least briefly addressed each area, and from these remarks the direction of his thought is clear. Others can now analyze these areas further.

John Paul's synthesis is apparent especially in the subject areas he treated exhaustively, in particular in the theology of the body. The theology of the body is a subjective, interior look at what happened to Adam and Eve in the garden of Eden before and after the first sin. The results of this examination of the experiences of our first parents are then applied to important areas related to sexuality, marriage, and family life.

The phenomenological method is also apparent in John Paul's work on the church entitled *Sources of Renewal*.[5] Written as a reflection on the church ten years after the opening of the Second Vatican Council, *Sources of Renewal* begins with the question the conciliar fathers put to themselves, "Church, what do you say of yourself?"[6] If the church can ask itself a question and, obviously, expect an answer, it is a personal subject—it is a person. In fact, the church is the mystical person of Christ.[7] As we have mentioned, every person has a self-awareness that contains the experiences that person has had. Since the church is the mystical person of Christ, it also has a self-awareness of its own acts. Therefore, the church can be studied as a subject, as a person, from within. In *Sources of Renewal*, the future pope endeavors to probe the church's self-awareness of its acts of knowing, that is, its faith and its self-awareness of its choices.

We find similar uses of the phenomenological method in most of the encyclicals and documents of John Paul II's papacy. The startling and exciting new way is present in the very first words of the very first encyclical: "The Redeemer of man, Jesus Christ, is the center of the universe and of history."[8] The same startling turn of phrase is found in other places in that encyclical, for instance, when John Paul teaches that man "is the primary and fundamental way for the Church."[9]

In *Laborem Exercens* (On Human Work),[10] the pope states that the primary purpose of work is the shaping of an individual into someone who acts like God, who participates in God's creative work by subduing the earth.[11] In working, human persons imitate God. They act as he acted when he "worked" to create the world. By acting as images of God through work, human persons shape themselves more and more into who they are: images of God. In this way, they fulfill themselves.

In *Familiaris Consortio,* John Paul's apostolic exhortation on the family, one of the headings in Part III is "Family, become what you are," and this phrase is also found in the body of the text.[12]

One of the pope's most interesting applications of the phenomenological method is his analysis of the parables of Christ and of the experiences of people with Christ. In his encyclical on morality, *Veritatis Splendor* (Splendor of Truth), John Paul examines the meeting of the rich young man with Christ.[13] He analyzes in great depth the experience of the young man in meeting Christ and argues that the young man's questions are the interior questions all of us have. The phenomenological method reveals something of human personhood when applied to the story of the rich young man. It reveals the deep questions we all have. But there is more here, because these meetings are with God himself. Thus, in meeting with the rich young man, Christ revealed the answers to the questions. We see in this use of Scripture the "double flow of data": human personhood is studied, and revelation answers the questions raised by that study.

We discover the same use of Scripture in John Paul's second encyclical, *Dives et Misericordia* (On the Mercy of God), where the pope has an extensive discussion of the parable of the prodigal son.[14] He analyzes the story from the point of view of the interior experiences of the prodigal, affirming that the prodigal's experiences are common to all of us. "That son . . . in a certain sense is the man of every period." The prodigal demands his inheritance from his father, moves away to a distant country, squanders his money, and is reduced to working as a hireling on a farm. Almost starving and wishing he could devour the food the pigs are given, the prodigal comes to his senses and decides to return to his father. At this point, John Paul writes that "the analogy turns clearly towards man's interior." The prodigal not only knows that he has squandered money but has an "awareness of squandered sonship," of the loss of his own dignity. The prodigal's return to his father is a personal experience of forgiveness, but it also contains important objective, revealed truths. Through a phenomenological study of this parable, John Paul offers us some new and surprising insights. Phenomenology allows us to probe experiences of people—and in the study of the Scriptures, to probe people's experiences of revelation—as well as to know the truths of revelation.

The new personalism of Pope John Paul II is without a doubt a brilliant solution to a problem that has plagued the church and its theology since the Renaissance and Reformation periods. The Renaissance focused on human beings in a way that was foreign to the Middle Ages. While it is something of a oversimplification, there is some truth in the statement that medieval thought began with God, and Renaissance thought began with human beings. The Protestant Reformation furthered the emphasis on individual human beings, and especially on the individual, with its insistence on the private interpretation of Scripture. The same tendency can be seen in the development of science and in the scientific method, which has its roots in the Renaissance. Science is based on observation of individual phenomena, that is, on experimentation and the recording of the data gleaned from experiments. Science and the scientific method so dominate society that people are loath to accept conclusions from principles. When an individual's real experience is cited, however, people tend to accept conclusions based on that event, since it is observable and individual. The focus on the individual is also one of the touchstones of democracy. The emphasis on the individual and freedom has its roots in the Renaissance, the Reformation, the rise of science, and the development of democracy. It results in a concept of the world that is subjective, inductive, and experiential. The subjective turn of John Paul II's new synthesis allows revelation to be taught to the world of the twenty-first century in its own language and categories.

1. See Weigel, *Witness to Hope*, p. 343.

2. See Rocco Buttiglione, *Karol Wojtyla: The Thought of the Man Who Became Pope John Paul II*, trans. Paolo Guietti and Francesca Murphy (Grand

Rapids, MI: William B. Eerdmans, 1997), p. 82.

3. See Genesis 1:26.

4. See TB, no. 3, p. 30 (1).

5. See Karol Wojtyla, *Sources of Renewal: The Implementation of Vatican II*, trans. P. S. Falla (New York: Harper and Row, 1980).

6. See Wojtyla, *Sources of Renewal*, p. 36.

7. See Hogan and LeVoir, *Faith for Today*, pp. 151–85.

8. See John Paul II, *Redemptor Hominis* (Redeemer of Man), March 4, 1979, 1.

9. See *Redemptor Hominis*, 14.

10. See John Paul II, *Laborem Exercens* (On Human Work), September 14, 1981.

11. See Genesis 1:28.

12. See John Paul II, *Familiaris Consortio* (Apostolic Exhortation on the Family), November 22, 1981, 17.

13. See John Paul II, *Veritatis Splendor* (Splendor of Truth), August 6, 1993, 6–25. For the story of the rich young man in the Scriptures, see Matthew 19:16-21, and its parallels, Mark 10:17-31 and Luke 18:18-30.

14. See John Paul II, *Dives in Misericordia* (On the Mercy of God), November 30, 1980, 5–6. For the story of the prodigal son, see Luke 15:11-32.

The Human Person
in the Garden *of* Eden

General Audience Addresses 1 to 23

A. INTRODUCTION: ADDRESSES 1 TO 4

John Paul II sees in the questions presented to Christ in the gospels questions that all people of every time and place would ask Christ if they had the chance. As John Paul writes, "We must put ourselves precisely in the position of Christ's interlocutors today."[1] One of the recurring themes in John Paul's works is that since we are all created in God's image and likeness, we do not know ourselves or how to act unless we know Christ, the God-man who reveals God to us. Christ answers our most profound questions—and he is the only one who can, because he alone "reveals man to man himself."[2] It is not surprising, then, that John Paul begins his theology of the body series with a question posed by the Pharisees to Christ: "Is it lawful for a man to divorce his wife for any cause whatever?" Christ responds by referring to "the beginning": "Have you not read that from the beginning the Creator 'made them male and female'?" Christ's reference to "the beginning" would have been clearly understood by the Pharisees as a quotation of the very first words of the first chapter of Genesis: "In the beginning. . . ."[3] John Paul also notes that Christ quotes not only the first chapter of Genesis: "male and female He created them," but also the second chapter of Genesis, "For this reason a man shall leave his father and mother and be joined to his wife."[4] John Paul takes his cue from these words of Christ and discusses the early chapters of Genesis.

If one rereads the first three chapters of Genesis, it is noteworthy that there are two different accounts of the creation of the world and of human beings. The first, in the first chapter of Genesis, is set in the seven-day format, with Adam and Eve created together toward the end of the sixth day. The second chapter of Genesis, beginning with the fourth verse, gives a second account of creation, with Adam created first and Eve created later. The first account, in the first chapter of Genesis, is often called the Elohist account because Elohim is the name for God used in this account. The second account, in the second chapter of Genesis, is older. It is called the Yahwist account because the name for God used in this account is the more ancient name, Yahweh.

John Paul repeatedly makes the point that the first account of creation, in the first chapter of Genesis, is "objective." One might say that it is an account of creation from the divine point of view. This account is a statement of the facts of creation: the what, where, when, and how of creation. It clearly distinguishes man from the world. In fact, in a startling phrase, the pope writes that "the Creator seems to halt before calling him into existence, as if he were pondering within himself to make a decision."[5] Man is different from the world, and the reference to the creation of human beings in the image of God separates all human beings from the rest of creation, from the world.

Of vital importance in John Paul II's system of thought is his reference to "value." As we have seen,[6] value is a phenomenological term. In part, John Paul's theology of the body addresses are an analysis of the experiences of Adam and Eve in order to show how they came to know values through their experiences. These values and norms existed objectively, they were given in creation; but they became known to Adam and Eve through their experiences.

We need to understand here that when John Paul II uses the word "subjective," he doesn't mean to contrast "subjective opinion" with "objective truth." He uses the term "subjective" to refer to the individual experiences we each have of the norms/values given by God in creation. We come to know these norms through our lived experience. The same norm is experienced in a different way by each of us, and we each internalize the objective norm in our own way. Therefore, the experience is subjective, that is, individual. But the norm itself is universal. For example, the commandment against stealing is an objective norm. A seven-year-old child might steal some money from his mother's purse. She reprimands him, and he experiences the norm through her admonition—and never forgets that experience. He has internalized the norm against stealing in a subjective way.

This point helps to clarify what John Paul is doing in his third talk when he speaks about the second account of creation. He describes it as "subjective" and "psychological."[7] In other words, it is the revelation of the truths of the first account of creation viewed through the lens of the individual experiences of Adam and Eve. As we have said previously,[8] John Paul uses the first chapter of Genesis, with its objective statement of the truths of creation, as a control on the subjective, experiential revelation of those same truths in the second chapter of Genesis.

The pope makes a vital point toward the end of the third address. He insists that by his reference to "the beginning," Christ is expecting us to "go beyond" the boundary caused by original sin. We are to live according to the original norm, even though we suffer the effects of original sin. One might ask how Christ could give such a command. He can give it because he is the one who carries the cross.[9] John Paul speaks in the fourth address of the "mystery of redemption." The redemption makes it possible for us to live as Adam and Eve did before sin, because through our redemption by the passion, death, and resurrection of Christ, we are blessed with divine life, that is, grace. Grace makes it possible—though not easy—to live as if original sin had not happened.

In the fourth address we should notice the third paragraph, where John Paul talks about two states of man: before and after sin. The pope explains that both of these states are present in man "in his inner self, in his knowledge, conscience, choice and decision."[10] This, of course, is another indication of the phenomenological method of analyzing the experiences of Adam and Eve "from the inside." The record of these experiences, recorded almost as a philosopher gathering data on human experiences would record them, is found in the second and third chapters of Genesis.

The third paragraph of the fourth address contains a reference to the "most ancient covenant." By this term, which is found in later addresses and is fundamental to John Paul's thought, the pope designates the covenant between Adam and God established in God's act of creation. A covenant is a union of love between God and man. In creating him, God expressed his love for Adam and, through Adam, for every single human being God would create. God is "being" itself. Love is the gift of oneself. In creating Adam, God shared being, or existence, with him and thus shared himself with Adam. He loved Adam. In return, Adam was grateful to God and implicitly undertook to return God's love. Adam and Eve broke this covenant with God when they sinned. Through sin the original covenant was annihilated, and the space between man and God was filled with evil.[11]

When the original covenant was broken by sin, human beings became subject to sin and its effects. John Paul uses the phrase "historical man" to refer to all of us who are subject to original sin. He stresses the point that it is impossible to understand our present state (the "historical" state) without reference to the previous state (the state of "original innocence"). Thus, a study of the experiences of Adam and Eve in paradise, that is, before sin, is essential.

This is particularly true, the pope insists, because by referring to "the beginning," Christ is expecting us to "go beyond" the boundary caused by original sin and live according to the original norm. Even though we suffer the effects of original sin, we are to live as though it had never occurred.

B. ADAM'S DISCOVERY OF HIMSELF THROUGH ORIGINAL SOLITUDE: ADDRESSES 5 TO 7

In the fifth address John Paul makes a fundamental point for the entire series. He teaches that when Adam was created alone, according to the second chapter of Genesis, he was called "man." In Hebrew, the word used for this was not "man" in the sense of a male human being, but rather the word meaning "man" in the sense of a human person, as though Adam when first created alone was neither male nor female. Created alone, Adam was alone. He experienced solitude and a certain loneliness. But this solitude was not simply the solitude of a male human being lacking a female human being; it was a solitude of being alone as a human being. There was no other human person yet in existence. Further, since Adam (a human being) experienced this solitude, the experience is common to all human persons, both men and women. This point is critical to the whole notion, developed later in the theology of the body, that the original experiences are the common inheritance of all human beings.

1. Adam's Discovery of His Mind

It is through Adam's experience of solitude that he begins to discover himself. In the second account of creation, Adam is created and then placed in the garden. He is given a task by God: to name the animals. [12] Up to this point in the second account of creation, Adam has been the object of God's activity. But with the naming of the animals, Adam is to act, and in acting, he will begin to know something of who he is. As John Paul explains, "The first meaning of man's original solitude is defined on the basis of a specific test or examination which man undergoes before God (and in a certain way also before himself). By means of this test, man becomes aware of his own superiority, that is, that he cannot be considered on the same footing as any other species of living beings on the earth."[13]

We need to pause at this quotation and explain how the pope can write that Adam's test is also "before himself." Phenomenology, the philosophical method the pope employs throughout his writings, uses our own self-awareness, our consciousness, as an entrance into the mystery of the human person.[14] Our consciousness has two functions. First, it has a memory function, inasmuch as it stores all of our previous acts. Simply put, we are aware of our actions; we can look back and see what we have done. Self-knowledge, then, develops through action. Second, our consciousness helps us determine who we are. In storing the awareness of our acts in the memory, consciousness allows us to become what we do. In other words, we become persons who do those activities. For as we act with an awareness of our actions, and as the self-awareness of our acts is stored in our consciousness, the acts become part of us. In this way, we constitute ourselves by our acts. The pope would say that we "determine ourselves."

The last paragraph of the fifth address applies these ideas to Adam's activity of naming the animals. "Man finds himself alone before God mainly to express, through a first self-definition, his own self-knowledge."[15] When we act, we become persons who do those activities, since, through our consciousness, our acts become part of us. We become what we do. We shape ourselves by our actions. At the same time, through our actions, we come to know who we are; we gain self-knowledge. Self-knowledge then develops through action. Adam acted, that is, he named the animals, and through this he came to know himself as one who named animals. His awareness of naming the animals revealed to Adam that he "possesses a cognitive faculty."[16] That is, he came to see that he is the only earthly creature God has created with a mind! As the pope writes, "Man is alone because he is 'different' from the visible world, from the world of living beings," because he has a mind.[17] Through the discovery of his mind, Adam is coming to know himself as a person, and also as the only person with a body in all of earthly creation.

One further point is interesting here. Before developing Adam's discovery of his own cognitive faculty, the pope writes an astounding line: "Created man finds himself before God as if . . . in search of his own entity."[18] Adam is trying to define himself by finding some other being like himself. In some ways, it is easier to recognize human personhood in someone else—at least at first. A baby discovers herself partly in and through interaction with parents, grandparents, brothers, sisters, and so on. But Adam finds no one like himself. Through that negative discovery, Adam knows that he is not like the visible world. He understands himself as a person—a being who has an inner life.

In differentiating himself from the visible world as one who has a mind, Adam realizes that he is a person. Since there is no other person in the visible world, Adam realizes that he is alone. This realization is what John Paul calls the *meaning* of original solitude. When the pope uses the word "meaning," he is employing it in a semitechnical sense. "Meaning" indicates the conclusions derived by a human person from an examination of the experiences contained within his or her consciousness. In other words, "meaning" is a person's subjective understanding. This definition will be very important as we continue to analyze the pope's thought. Adam named the animals and had an awareness, a consciousness, of this act. By examining his consciousness, which contained this experience, he came to know himself as different from the animals, because they obviously did not have this consciousness of their own acts. As a result, he came to know himself as a person who was alone. This knowledge is the "meaning" of solitude.

2. Adam's Discovery of His Body and His Power to Choose

In the sixth address the pope analyzes how Adam, from his own experiences of acting, knew that God had made him as a person in the image and likeness of himself. John Paul observes that when God warns Adam not to eat the fruit of the tree of knowledge of good and evil, the man was confronted with the possibility of choosing. He could either follow what God had said or not follow it. Through God's presenting him with the possibility of choosing, Adam came to know his power to choose; he discovered his will. Thus, through solitude he knew himself as a person with the powers of thinking and choosing. This was a self-discovery—knowledge gleaned through self-knowledge. The pope is analyzing how Adam, from his own experiences of acting, knew that God had made him as a person in the image and likeness of himself, that is, in the image and likeness of God.

The remainder of the sixth address makes the point that the experiences of naming of the animals and of confronting the tree of knowledge of good and evil, through which Adam discovers that he is a person, were not just interior experiences but happened precisely through his body. With his bodily eyes, Adam saw the animals and the tree of knowledge of good and evil. The ancient text even has Adam hearing God (with his bodily ears). Therefore, the self-knowledge gained of himself as a person came through his body. In other words, the body revealed to him who he was. Our bodies reveal ourselves to others and even to our own selves.

The powers of thinking and choosing, as well as the abilities of the human body, are also revealed by the human activity that the second chapter of Genesis mentions—"tilling the soil"—the reason for the creation of man in the first place. Only a person with a body could do this. "Tilling the soil" is purposeful work, requiring knowledge in the mind to know what to do, a choice in the will to do it, and a body to undertake the work. Adam discovered not just that he was a person with a mind and a will; he also discovered "the meaning of his own corporality."[19] The meaning of original solitude was the discovery by Adam that he was a person with a mind, will, and body and that there was no other being like him on the earth.

a. The Human Body as the Expression of the Human Person

The seventh address expands on Adam's discovery of the meaning of his own body. Here John Paul uses for the first time the famous line that is identified with the entire theology of the body series: "The body expresses the person."[20] As John Paul remarks, "The body, and it alone, is capable of making visible what is invisible: the spiritual and the divine. It was created to transfer into the visible reality of the world the mystery hidden since time immemorial in God, and thus be a sign of it."[21]

The human body, then, is more than the sum of its biological parts. Through the body, with its apparently understandable biological functions, human personhood is revealed. The human body is the only creation of God that expresses and manifests in a visible way a spiritual reality: personhood. The angels are persons and so are the three Persons in God, but none of these can express or make visible their persons. That is left, by the design of God, to human beings, who are the only persons with bodies. It is true that Jesus made his person visible, but he was able to do this by assuming a human nature with a body. It was as a man, a human being, that he was able to reveal himself in and through his body. Therefore it is true that only human beings are capable of manifesting personhood in the visible world.

Our bodies manifest our persons, and since we are images of God, our bodies, by manifesting our persons, actually reveal something of who God is. How could it be otherwise? God created human beings in his image and likeness. Human beings have bodies that reveal who they are: images of God. When you see a living human body, you see a visible expression of an image of God. When you see an image of God, you see something of God himself. In expressing our own persons and in manifesting God, the human body is a unique creation of God, full of immeasurable value and dignity. Human beings are truly a "little less than God."[22] This is the truth Adam came to realize in discovering the meaning of his body.

b. Is the Human Body a Machine?

Since the human body expresses our persons, it can be said to speak the "language of personhood."[23] But many in our society would accept a contrary view: that the body is something like a machine. This view is reinforced through some science-fiction movies and television shows that treat machines as if they were persons. The popular *Star Wars* series has two robots, C3PO and R2D2. Both of these robots are portrayed as persons in machinelike bodies. Yet both of them have personalities. R2D2 reacts emotionally by jumping up and down or spinning around when good news arrives for his masters. But machines cannot really have an emotional reaction. For example, a computer does not react emotionally when a pleasant e-mail is received. The character named Data on *Star Trek: The Next Generation* is also a machine portrayed as a person. In fact, in one of the episodes, Data is defined as a unique life-form! Data violates the so-called "duck principle": if it looks like a duck, quacks like a duck, and swims like a duck, it is a duck. Data looks like a person, acts like a person, and talks like a person, but he is actually an android. A corollary of viewing a machine as a person is viewing the human body as a machine. The *Robocop* movies demonstrate the premise that a human being can become a machine and still retain some of his or her personhood. *The Six Million Dollar Man* television series was about a test pilot, Steve Austin, who was destroyed in an airplane crash but is then rebuilt. The head of the agency that rebuilds Austin says at the beginning of every show, "We can make him better than he was." The "bettering" of Steve Austin is accomplished with bionics—computer chips and machinelike parts that give him superhuman powers. The implication is that the human body is just a collection of parts, a machine, that can be rebuilt to be even better.

A similar message is often conveyed by sportscasters who, in the attempt to give information quickly and succinctly, sometimes speak of the athletes as though they were machines: "She has all the tools!" "He has great wheels!" "He has an arm like a rifle."

Probably most of us sometimes refer to our own bodies with machinelike references: "The plumbing is not working so well. I need to have it looked at!" "The old ticker needs new spark plugs!" "I need to have the pipes cleaned out!" "I cannot remember as much any more because my disk is full and it takes longer to access!" Even references to food as fuel or to coffee as "leaded" imply that the body has machinelike qualities.

Of course, there is nothing immoral about watching science fiction movies or listening to sportscasts in which athletes are referred to as machines. And without question there is nothing sinful about referring to our own bodies, and especially medical difficulties, using machinelike metaphors. A real difficulty arises, however, when we actually *believe* that our bodies are machines. Some people in our society do actually accept this view of the body/person structure. It is on the basis of this view that some use the line "It's my body" to justify procured abortion. The meaning is clear: "I own my body the way I own a machine. Like a machine, I can do what I wish with it or to it."

If the body were a machine, it could be owned and used. It would be possible, perhaps even desirable, to manipulate the body for one's own purposes. For example, the body could be the means of highs achieved through the use of alcohol or drugs. If the sexual organs were only machine parts, the owner would have a right to use them for any purpose he or she wanted. If an individual wished to use his or her sexual devices to achieve a sexual high, for example, by masturbation, it would be his or her right as an owner to do so. Furthermore, owners can alter machines at will. So if the body were a machine that was owned, it could be changed. Thus, tubal ligations, vasectomies, and contraception would be justifiable.

Some would applaud these viewpoints, arguing that our bodies are indeed machines that we own and can manipulate as we wish. However, if the body were a thing, a machine, for the purposes of sterilization, abortion, or contraception, it would be a machine always and in every other instance also. Terrible consequences would follow. For example, machines are bought and sold. If the body were a machine that is owned, it could be bought or sold. We usually call such trafficking in human flesh slavery, and we have made every effort to abolish it. If the body were a thing separate from its "owner," there would be nothing wrong with renting it, just as cars are rented. That, in fact, is what prostitution is, and most civilizations have outlawed it. In fact, if our bodies were machines, then any interaction between two people in and through their bodies would be the same as two machines touching or two computers linked together through a server. Such interactions would have nothing to do with the "persons," therefore, but would only involve their bodies. As most people would acknowledge, such approaches to human relations would be absurd. They have been rejected for centuries by most civilizations, at least in thought and word if not always in practice.

By arguing forcefully that the human body is the "expression of the person," John Paul is asserting the only possible alternative to the thesis that the human body is a machine. As an expression of the person, the human body participates in the dignity and value given by God to all human persons when God created us in his image and likeness. In effect, John Paul is holding the only possible view of human personhood, because the alternative is unthinkable. We cannot even entertain the possibility of allowing the body to be bought and sold, rented and used. The case for civilization demands that the human body be respected and valued as it should be, that is, as the expression of a human person.

c. Adam and the Death of the Body

The remainder of the seventh address is a discussion of what Adam might have understood by death. This notion is introduced when God says that if Adam were to eat the fruit of the tree of knowledge of good and evil, he would surely die. As a counterpoint to Adam's self-discovery so far, the discussion of how Adam could have perceived the meaning of death is very interesting. The pope seems to question whether Adam, lacking any experience of death, could have known what this truly meant. Nevertheless, the warning by God of the possibility of death clearly indicates to Adam, even with his limited understanding, that he is not the same as God. God cannot die, because God is being itself. Adam was not being itself. He *could* die; his body could return to dust.

3. Conclusion of Addresses 5 to 7

Through the experience of solitude, Adam (who at this stage is humanity, not yet distinguished as male and female) knows himself as a person with the powers of thinking and choosing. He knows that his body is the outward, visible manifestation of his interior personhood, of what he thinks and what he chooses. Since he knows himself as an embodied person and has heard God's warning that he will surely be doomed to die if he eats the fruit of the tree of knowledge, he also knows that his body can die, can cease to have life. "Right from the outset the alternative between death and immortality enters the definition of man. It belongs 'from the beginning' to the meaning of his solitude before God himself."[24]

C. ADAM AND EVE'S DISCOVERY OF THEMSELVES THROUGH ORIGINAL UNITY: ADDRESSES 8 TO 10

In the eighth talk we read that "the meaning of 'original solitude,' which can be referred simply to 'man,' is substantially prior to the meaning of original unity."[25] Having experienced solitude, Adam knows himself, has an awareness of himself as a being who thinks, chooses, and manifests himself in the visible world through his flesh and blood. But he is alone. Then God puts Adam to sleep and forms the first woman, Eve. "The analogy of sleep indicates . . . a specific return to non-being. . . . That is, it indicates a return to the moment preceding the creation, in order that, through God's creative initiative, solitary 'man' may emerge from it again in his double unity as male and female."[26] Man, who has had the experience of solitude and has come to know himself, sleeps and then emerges from the sleep as two. But both of the two have experienced solitude. Eve, as another human person, shared with Adam the common experience of solitude, because solitude belongs to Adam as human person, not as male person. The experience of solitude belongs, as it were, to humanity. Eve, together with Adam, had the benefit of the experience of solitude, so she, too, had come to the realization of who she was as a person with self-awareness of mind, will, and body.

1. "This at Last Is Bone of My Bones"

Adam's cry of joy is well known: "This one, at last, is bone of my bones and flesh of my flesh."[27] Humanity "awakens from his sleep as 'male and female.'"[28] The pope writes about this line, "If it is possible to read impressions and emotions through words so remote, one might also venture to say that the depth and force of this first and 'original' emotion of the male-man in the presence of the humanity of the woman, and at the same time in the presence of the femininity of the other human being, seems something unique and unrepeatable."[29] Adam recognizes in Eve another whose body expresses a person.[30] Seeing that she is the same as he in her humanity, he recognizes personhood in her—as she does in him.

Adam implicitly understood that something was lacking in solitude. In naming the animals, he did not find one like himself. With the creation of Eve, solitude is overcome. This is the reason for the cry of inexpressible joy: "This one, at last, is bone of my bones and flesh of my flesh." Only through the creation of a helper "fit for him" can Adam surpass "the limit of man's solitude."[31] In both Adam and Eve there is a recognition of a mutual belonging: they belong to one another in a way that they do not belong to the rest of the visible creation and the living bodies it contains.

There is also a sense of a reciprocity between them. Indispensable for this reciprocity was their self-knowledge: "all that constituted the foundation of the solitude of each of them. . . . Self-knowledge and self-determination, that is, subjectivity and consciousness of the meaning of one's own body, was also indispensable."[32] The union of Adam and Eve "could be formed only on the basis of a 'double solitude' of man and of woman, that is, as their meeting in their distinction from the world of living beings (*animalia*), which gave them both the possibility of being and existing in a special reciprocity."[33] The pope means that through the discovery in solitude that the human person—mind, will, and body—was radically different from the other living, bodied beings in the world, Adam and Eve could see one another as human beings who were both persons. Without the discovery in solitude of the radical difference between human persons and animals, Adam and Eve would not have recognized themselves as unique and belonging to each other.

2. Masculinity and Femininity

In a particularly forceful remark, John Paul writes, "These are, as it were, two 'incarnations' of the same metaphysical solitude before God and the world—two ways, as it were, of 'being a body' and at the same time a man, which complete each other—two complementary dimensions of self-consciousness and self-determination and, at the same time, two complementary ways of being conscious of the meaning of the body."[34]

Of Eve, John Paul says, "The creation takes place almost simultaneously in two dimensions: the action of God-Yahweh who creates occurs in correlation with the process of human consciousness."[35] In Genesis 2:18, God says that it is not good for the man to be alone. In his self-discovery through original solitude, Adam came to realize this—a realization implied by the statement in Genesis 2:20 that in naming the animals no suitable partner was found for man. In 2:21, Adam is cast into sleep, and the two emerge. "There is no doubt that man falls into that 'sleep' with the desire of finding a being like himself."[36]

God knew that it was not good for man to be alone. Man, having discovered this truth in naming the animals, desires another, a second self. When man becomes aware of that desire, God acts. How could man's dignity be more respected? God did not just act; like any good parent or teacher, he waited until man was prepared. And, of course, the result was the cry of joy recorded in Genesis. John Paul also makes the point that it is only after the emergence from his "sleep" that the original human being becomes a "man" in the sense of a male, a masculine person. Clearly, there could be no masculine until there was a feminine.

We are called by our very being to love as God loves and to express that love in and through the body. Can you imagine life if Eve had not been created? The man, one human person without sexual differentiation, created alone and remaining in that situation, would have been the most frustrated of creatures. Although created to love as God loves and to express that love through his body, such a loving act would be impossible for him because there would be no means of expressing his love with another human person in and through a human body. One might even say it would have been cruel of God to leave any human being alone without the possibility of doing what human beings were created to do!

3. How Human Persons Image God

Adam saw Eve, and she saw him. They knew from their very first gaze that they were called to love one another. As human persons, we are each images of God. Adam in solitude before the creation of Eve was an image of God; Eve was also an image of God. But, created in God's image, we are called by God from the very nature of our being as images of God to act as he does. When we act as God acts, that is, when we love, we reflect him not just by our existence, but also by what we do. In this sense, we become images of God by loving as he loves. We shape, or determine, ourselves more and more by acting as images of God, that is, by loving. Nevertheless, in our very being as persons, even before loving as God loves, we are images of God.

It is as though there are two ways we image God, and the first way is an absolute requirement for the second. First, we are created as persons. It is necessary to be a person, an image of God, in order to act like him. Second, when we act as God does, that is, when we love, we become more and more the image of God; we become more and more what we are. "Man became the 'image and likeness' of God not only through his own humanity"—that is, through his being as a person—"but also through the communion of persons which man and woman form right from the beginning."[37]

A communion of persons is a loving union of two or more people. This union is founded on knowledge and choice. Adam and Eve knew one another as persons. And they clung to one another[38] by their free choice, in and through their wills. By knowing one another as persons through their minds, by choosing in their wills to give themselves to one another in love, and by expressing that knowledge and choice in and through their bodies, through the differences of masculinity and femininity, Adam and Eve formed a communion of persons. This union of love was an imitation of the divine love found within the Trinity. In the Trinity, the three Persons of God know one another and choose to donate themselves totally to one another in a perfect self-gift that creates a communion of persons. Of course, the divine communion is absolutely perfect, whereas the communion between Adam and Eve, even before sin, was not perfect. Nevertheless, the communion of persons formed by Adam and Eve was a reflection—an image—of the divine communion in the Godhead.

D. ADAM AND EVE'S DISCOVERY OF THE NUPTIAL MEANING OF THEIR BODIES: ADDRESSES 11 TO 15

In address 11 John Paul reminds us that the experiences he calls the "original" ones, that is, solitude, unity, and nakedness, are "at the root of every human experience." They are part of all of us and belong to man's "theological prehistory."[39] The understanding of each of these original experiences depends on the previous one. Solitude, the first experience, can be understood on its own, but unity depends on a proper appreciation of solitude, and the understanding of nakedness depends on a comprehension of both solitude and unity. In addition, each of these experiences is known in man's self-awareness, his consciousness, through his body.

1. Nakedness

The pope makes this last point explicit when he remarks that "the sentence, according to which the first human beings, man and woman, 'were naked' and yet 'were not ashamed,' unquestionably describes their state of consciousness, in fact, their mutual experience of the body."[40] Notice the pope's reference to their "consciousness." The experience of nakedness for

Adam and Eve before sin is contrasted with their experience of nakedness after sin, when their eyes were opened and "they knew they were naked, and they sewed fig leaves together and made themselves aprons."[41] Unlike solitude and unity, nakedness has a "before" and "after." Adam and Eve's experience of their nakedness before one another, as the pope might say, changes after sin. Therefore, nakedness is a boundary experience: it points to the change in the human person caused by sin. Further, nakedness after sin cannot be understood without reference to nakedness before sin.

2. Shame

In the twelfth address, John Paul explains a little of what shame is, because shame is connected with nakedness after sin. Then he teaches that Adam and Eve's lack of shame is not a deprivation or a sign of a more primitive state of humanity but rather points to a "particular fullness of consciousness and experience."[42] He then briefly summarizes the experiences of solitude and unity. The last point in this address is fundamental: the "fullness of consciousness and experience" that Adam and Eve knew in their mutual nakedness was that their bodies manifested their persons and, more particularly, that their bodies manifested their choice to give themselves to each other in a communion of persons, that is, in a unity of love.

In address 13, we learn that only persons can give themselves, because only persons can make choices based on knowledge. Such a choice could be an act of will to make a gift of oneself. God gave himself to Adam and Eve when he created the world. They understood this gift in creation, and, as persons, they were capable of making a choice to give themselves to each other and to God.

3. The Nuptial Meaning of the Body

Adam and Eve were created as gifts for one another. Their visible bodies manifested this truth. In fact, it was through their masculinity and femininity that they could bodily express their gift to one another. Further, their creation as gift for one another manifested and made visible in the created order the gift of God when he created the world. Their consciousness, their self-awareness that they were created as gifts for one another, manifested in and through their differences as man and woman, that is, through their being masculine and feminine, is what the pope calls the "nuptial meaning of the body."[43] The nuptial meaning of the body is a key concept in the theology of the body addresses, and one to which the pope will return again and again.

In its masculinity and femininity, the human body is the visible sign and the means of the human person's self-donation in love to another. Original nakedness is of critical importance, therefore, because it leads Adam and Eve and all of us, because their original experiences are part of all of us as our theological prehistory, to understand the nuptial meaning of our own bodies. Speaking of the first pages of the Book of Genesis, John Paul says, "Awareness of the meaning of the body that is derived from them—in particular of its nuptial meaning—is the fundamental element of human existence in the world."[44]

Awareness of the nuptial meaning of the body—the fact that we are created to love and be loved—is the fundamental truth about human beings because it is central to all human life worth living. As John Paul taught in his first encyclical, "Man cannot live without love. He remains a being that is incomprehensible for himself, his life is senseless if love is not revealed to him, if he does not experience it and make it his own, if he does not participate intimately in it."[45] This is naturally so, because every human person is created in the image and likeness of God and thus is called to do what God does, that is, to love and be loved. The subjective discovery of this truth is what John Paul means when he speaks of the "nuptial meaning of the body."

4. Love, the Essential Activity of the Human Person

In the fifteenth address John Paul quotes a famous passage from the *Pastoral Constitution on the Church in the Modern World* of the Second Vatican Council: "The last Council . . . declared that man is the only creature in the visible world that God willed 'for its own sake.' It then added that man 'can fully discover his true self only in a sincere giving of himself.'"[46] These points are obvious if we remember that we are created in God's image. As images of God, we are called by our very being, by our very humanity to do what God does, that is, to love as he loves. An image does what it is an image of. When someone looks in a mirror and combs his or her hair, the image in the mirror "combs its hair." If God loves, we, as his images, that is, as reflections of him, are called to love. This calling, this task, so to speak, assigned to man in creation by God, is manifested in the human body precisely through the differences in masculinity and femininity. Each person is able to come to an awareness that his or her body manifests God's call to love as he loves and to express that love in and through the body. At the same time, each of us as an individual is created for his or her own sake. We are not things created for something else. We are created to be a gift in love, through our own free choice, to other persons. Only by mirroring God's activity in this way do we act as we should. If we act this way, we become more and more who we are: images of God. This is the fundamental truth about us as human persons.

Before sin, in paradise, Adam and Eve had a clear perception of this truth through the experience of their own nakedness. They also had the ability to fulfill their understanding of this truth by loving each other, giving themselves to each other and accepting each other's gift of self. The human perception of this truth as well as the ability to act on it were terribly marred by sin. In fact, it is impossible for historical man simply to cross back over the threshold revealed by the boundary of nakedness.

We can never attain the state that Adam and Eve had in paradise. With the help of Christ and the redemption of the body, that is, through divine grace, it has become possible for us to love as we should and to express that self-donation in and through our bodies, but only with a struggle. This aspect of the state of historical man, that is, of all human beings after Adam and Eve (except for Christ and Mary, the mother of Christ), the pope leaves to the second cycle of the theology of the body.

E. ORIGINAL INNOCENCE: THE STATE OF ADAM AND EVE BEFORE SIN: ADDRESSES 16 TO 19

1. Original Innocence

In addresses 16 to 19 we find an examination of Adam and Eve's interior state before sin. Their interior state was different from our own, because they were not yet affected by the sin of which we are the heirs. Because of their interior state, they were able to perceive and accept the nuptial meaning of the body and then act on this truth by giving themselves completely to each other in authentic love, that is, in love that mirrors God's love.

John Paul derives this teaching from Genesis 2:25: "The man and his wife were both naked, yet they felt no shame." The pope writes that this immunity from shame "directs us toward the mystery of man's original innocence. It is a mystery of his existence, prior to the knowledge of good and evil and almost 'outside' it."[47] The lack of shame in Adam and Eve points to the fact that their interior state was one of innocence.

"The body itself is, in a way, an 'eyewitness' of this characteristic."[48] While this may be a poetic way of saying it, what the pope means here is that Adam and Eve were before one another naked and were not embarrassed, because their innocence allowed them to see one another in the full truth of their existence—the truth that each was a gift to the other. The body is an "eyewitness" of this inner state because the lack of shame is directly related to their physical characteristics, to their bodies, and more specifically, to the differences in their masculinity and femininity.

Their state of innocence is what enabled them to discover the nuptial meaning of their bodies. Speaking of Genesis 2:25, John Paul writes, "It is essential that the discovery of the nuptial meaning of the body, which we read in the testimony of Genesis, takes place through original innocence."[49] In other words, without original innocence, the realization that they were created as gifts for one another, that is, to love one another as God loves, would have been impossible.

Adam and Eve could not have perceived the nuptial meaning of their bodies and acted in accordance with that truth if their wills had not chosen to acknowledge this meaning of their bodies. But to be able to choose to accept this truth, it was necessary that they be innocent, that is, without shame. As the pope writes, this discovery of the nuptial meaning of the body "reveals and highlights"[50] original innocence, because without original innocence they could have never accepted the nuptial meaning of their bodies. Without original innocence, they would have been inclined not to give themselves to one another but rather to try to take or possess one another.[51] They would have treated one another as objects to be used rather than as persons to be loved.[52]

In the last substantive paragraph of address 16, we read that original innocence is a particular "purity of heart."[53] Through this purity, Adam and Eve were able to choose to see each other in the full truth of their existence, that is, that they were created as gifts for one another.

In address 17 the pope goes on to say that what Adam chose through original innocence was to see Eve as a person created for her own sake, not as a thing for his own use. Eve chose to view Adam in the same way. Thus, "the innocence 'of the heart,' and consequently, the innocence of the experience, means a moral participation in the eternal and permanent act of God's will."[54] That is, Adam and Eve saw in each other what God had created, and they chose in their wills to view one another as God viewed them—beings possessing an infinite dignity and value.

2. Adam and Eve: Gifts for One Another

Adam and Eve gave themselves to each other and accepted the other's gift in accordance with this God-given dignity and value that each possessed as a being created for his or her own sake. And since they were created not only for their own sakes but also to be loving gifts for one another, when they gave themselves and received each other, they acted in accordance with their very being: they acted as images of God. John Paul writes about Eve (he says the same thing in a slightly different way about Adam a little later) that through her gift of self, expressed through her femininity in all of its aspects, "she reaches the inner depth of her person and full possession of herself."[55]

In her self-giving, Eve reaches the "inner depth of her person," because she acts in accordance with who she is: a person created to love as God loves. There is no more profound human act than authentic love, because we are created in God's image and likeness to do what he does. Love is *the* act of God, and therefore it is *the* act of a human person. She has "full possession of herself," because she consciously chooses to love and because her whole being acts in accordance with her choice. Further, this act is "contained" in her consciousness. And, by determining herself as a lover through the act of authentic, self-giving love, she constitutes herself as a lover in accordance with the way God made her. She not only acknowledges in her mind that she is created in God's image, but, by choosing to act in accordance with the way God made her, she participates in her own creation as an image of God—obviously in a secondary sense, because she is not creating herself out of nothing, an act that is impossible for anyone except God.

In address 18 John Paul stresses that while original innocence is not recoverable today, there remains in all of us an echo of it—an intimation that all of us are called to see one another in the full truth of the dignity and value that each of us possesses. This is John Paul's way of restating the personalistic norm that he laid down in *Love and Responsibility*, written almost twenty years before the theology of the body: "The person is a good towards which the only proper and adequate attitude is love."[56]

In the last paragraph of address 19 the pope summarizes in a dramatic and almost poetic fashion the points he has previously made. "Genesis 2:23-25," he writes, "narrates the first feast of humanity in all the original fullness of the experience of the nuptial meaning of the body. It is a feast of humanity, which draws its origin from the divine sources of truth and love in the mystery of creation."[57] It is a feast of humanity because it is a feast of love.

F. KNOWLEDGE AND PROCREATION: ADDRESSES 20 TO 22

In address 20 John Paul takes up a different topic: knowledge and procreation. Both of these concepts are connected with fertility, which, in turn, is connected with the creation of Adam and Eve as male and female. Therefore, this new discussion, the pope notes, remains within the context of the creation of Adam and Eve and their original innocence.

Quoting Genesis 4:1 in a translation that renders the Hebrew form of the verb "to know" (*yada*) literally—"Adam knew his wife and she conceived and bore Cain"—the pope notes that this ancient mode of expression reveals a depth of meaning that sometimes goes unnoticed. The term "to know" directs us to the dimension of personhood, for only a person with a mind can possibly know. When Adam "knew" his wife, he was acting as a person. Therefore, the sexual union is not simply a result of instinct or nature but is a personal act, an act of knowing. In addition, the act of knowing points to a choice in the will. Before we learn something, that is, gain knowledge, we must choose to learn, choose to know. Only persons are capable of choosing (an act of the will) to know (an act of the mind). Further, while the Scriptures speak of Adam knowing Eve, Eve also knew Adam.

1. We Can Know a Human Person by Reading the Language of the Body

As the expression of the person, the human body speaks a language, the language of personhood. Further, since each of us is a unique and unrepeatable individual, each of our bodies expresses our own personhood, our own unique reflection of God. Thus, while all of our bodies speak with the same grammar and vocabulary, each body speaks in a way that expresses our unique, individual identity. Part of that unique personal identity is our masculinity and femininity. Thus, when Adam and Eve knew each other in the sexual union, they "read" the language of the other's body and came to know the personal language the other's body spoke.

It is important to notice the pope's phrase that Adam and Eve are given to each other as a "subject."[58] John Paul uses the word "subject" as a technical term in his philosophical system. A subject is a person who consciously makes a decision to act in a certain way. This decision is then contained in the person's self-awareness, in his or her consciousness. As personal subjects, Adam and Eve chose to know each other in the sexual union. Thus they acted as subjects, shaping themselves into husband and wife. They could then gaze internally on their consciousness and see that they had come to be husband and wife.

2. Adam and Eve Knew Each Other through Procreation

Toward the beginning of address 21 the pope adds the thought that the knowledge Adam and Eve gained through their sexual union involved "a further discovery" of the meaning of the body. This further discovery completes a process that began in original solitude, when the man discovered through his body that, unlike the animals, he was a person. The process continued in original unity, when, through the mutual discovery of bodily masculinity and femininity, Adam and Eve discovered that they were called to love one another. Now, through the sexual union, Adam and Eve discover the procreative meaning of their bodies. And it is in procreation that the full truth, the full meaning of the language of the body is revealed. Through conception and birth, the man sees his wife as mother and she sees him as father.

It would be a grave error to see in conception and birth simply biological processes. There is much more going on, because conception and birth are included in the act of knowing: "Adam knew his wife," and she conceived. In the conjugal union, Adam and Eve choose to know one another, to read the full meaning expressed in the language of their bodies. The truth of their bodies, discovered subjectively—that is, through their experiences—includes their potential as parents, their capacity to become a father and a mother.

In addition to discovering fatherhood and motherhood, Adam and Eve discover themselves again in their recognition of the humanity of their child. In fatherhood and motherhood, Adam and Eve discover the full truth that their bodies speak, and they also see themselves again in the child.

A final point of address 21 is that Eve is fully aware that the creation of the child is not the act of herself and her husband alone. She specifically acknowledges that she has conceived and given birth "with the help of the Lord."[59]

There is an interesting phrase toward the beginning of the next address (22). John Paul writes that through the conjugal union, through their choice to read the truth of the language of their bodies and know this truth, Adam and Eve "take possession" of their humanity.[60] John Paul means here that by knowing and loving in accordance with who they are, that is, persons made in the image and likeness of God, they determine themselves more and more to be images of God. They become who they are.

3. The Gift of Procreation Remains, Despite Sin

The remainder of address 22 reminds us that the possibility of motherhood and fatherhood, that is, human fertility, has been affected by sin. Childbirth is painful because of sin, and the prospect of death now haunts the giving of life, because each life on earth comes to an earthly end. "Awareness of the meaning of the body and awareness of its generative meaning come into contact, in man, with awareness of death, the inevitable horizon of which they bear within them. Yet the 'knowledge-generation' cycle always returns in human history. In it, life struggles ever anew with the inexorable perspective of death, and always overcomes it."[61] This line is reminiscent of the text of the nuptial blessing pronounced by the priest over the newly married couple at their wedding: "Father, by your plan man and woman are united, and married life has been established as the one blessing that was not forfeited by original sin or washed away by the flood."[62]

There is no better way to conclude this reflection than to quote the last words of the pope in this address: "In spite of all the experiences of his life, in spite of suffering, disappointment with himself, his sinfulness, and, finally, in spite of the inevitable prospect of death, man always continues to put knowledge at the beginning of generation. In this way, he seems to participate in that first 'vision' of God himself: God the Creator 'saw . . . and behold, it was very good.' And, ever anew, he confirms the truth of these words."[63]

G. CONCLUSION OF THE FIRST CYCLE: ADDRESS 23

The pope reminds us of Christ's reference to "the beginning" in his answer to the Pharisees' question on divorce. Their question continues to be asked by many today. The question pertained not just to divorce, but to the mystery of marriage and procreation. Questions about marriage and procreation, John Paul tells us, were addressed to the Second Vatican Council, and especially to Pope Paul VI, before he issued his famous encyclical letter, *Humanae Vitae* (On Human Life), the so-called "birth control encyclical." The Pharisees' question and those addressed to the church today cannot be answered without what John Paul calls a "total vision of man," which is what Christ gave us in his teaching. But this total vision of man needs to be probed and fleshed out—which is, of course, exactly the pope's project in the theology of the body.

John Paul contrasts the total vision of man with the many and varied partial understandings of humanity proposed in modern culture. Almost every academic discipline contributes something to the understanding of the human being: medical science, sociology, history, and so on. But only Christ, by revealing the Father, gives us the complete vision. Without that revelation, we would not know who we are or how we should act, because, as images of God, we do not know ourselves and how to act unless we know God, and Jesus reveals God. Included in his complete vision of man is the body. "The fact that theology also considers the body should not astonish or surprise anyone who is aware of the mystery and reality of the Incarnation. . . . Through the fact that the Word of God became flesh, the body entered theology through the main door."[64] There could hardly be a more succinct explanation of the basis for a theology of the body!

John Paul concludes by reminding his listeners that he still has two more "words" of Christ on marriage to consider: Christ's word about "looking lustfully," from the Sermon on the Mount, and his word about marriage and resurrection, which was the content of his response to the Sadducees when they asked him about marriage in heaven.

1. See TB, no. 1, p. 26 (4).

2. See John Paul II, *Redemptor Hominis*, 1, as well as Second Vatican Council, *Gaudium et Spes* (Pastoral Constitution on the Church in the Modern World), December 7, 1965, 22.

3. See Genesis 1:1.

4. For this entire dialogue between the Pharisees and Christ, see Matthew 19:3-9.

5. See TB, no. 2, p. 28 (3).

6. See above, Prologue, p. 26.

7. See TB, no. 3, p. 30 (1).

8. See above, Prologue, p. 29.

9. See Karol Wojtyla, *Sign of Contradiction* (New York: Seabury Press, 1979), pp. 190–91. This is a reference to one of the lines from John Paul's meditation on the eighth station in the Stations of the Cross. The meditation on the Stations was part of a retreat Cardinal Karol Wojtyla—the future John Paul II—preached to Pope Paul VI and Vatican officials at the beginning of Lent in 1976. The Stations have been reprinted in other versions.

10. See TB, no. 4, p. 32 (1).

11. See John Paul II, *Salvifici Doloris* (On the Christian Meaning of Human Suffering), February 11, 1984, 17.

12. See Genesis 2:5.

13. See TB, no. 5, p. 36 (4).

14. See above, Prologue, pp. 24–25.

15. See TB, no. 5, p. 37 (6).

16. See TB, no. 5, p. 37 (6).

17. See TB, no. 5, p. 37 (6).

18. See TB, no. 5, p. 36 (5).

19. See TB, no. 6, p. 39 (4).

20. See TB, no. 7, p. 41 (2).

21. See TB, no. 19, p. 76 (4).

22. See Psalm 8:5.

23. See *Familiaris Consortio*, 32.

24. See TB, no. 7, p. 42 (4).

25. See TB, no. 8, p. 43 (1).

26. See TB, no. 8, p. 44 (3).

27. See Genesis 2:23.

28. See TB, no. 8, p. 44 (3).

29. See TB, no. 9, p. 102 (1). John Paul's theology is certainly a theology for poets. The books and writings on physics by Stephen Hawking have been called "physics for poets" because of his scientifically accurate but marvelous descriptions of the cosmos. I would like to suggest that in the theology of the body series, John Paul II has written word paintings of the human person and marital love that can accurately be described as "theology for poets"!

30. See TB, no. 14, p. 61 (4).

31. See TB, no. 10, p. 50 (2).

32. See TB, no. 9, p. 46 (2).

33. See TB, no. 9, p. 46 (2).

34. See TB, no. 10, p. 48 (1).

35. See TB, no. 8, p. 43 (2).

36. See TB, no. 8, p. 44 (3).

37. See TB, no. 9, p. 46 (3).

38. See Genesis 2:24.

39. See TB, no. 11, p. 51 (1).

40. See TB, no. 11, p. 52 (3).

41. See Genesis 3:7.

42. See TB, no. 12, p. 55 (2).

43. See TB, no. 14, p. 62 (6).

44. See TB, no. 15, p. 66 (5).

45. See *Redemptor Hominis*, 12.

46. See TB, no. 15, p. 63 (1), and *Gaudium et Spes*, 24.

47. See TB, no. 16, p. 67 (3).

48. See TB, no. 16, p. 68 (3).

49. See TB, no. 16, p. 68 (3).

50. See TB, no. 16, p. 68 (3).

51. See below, Cycle 2, pp. 78–81.

52. See TB, no 19, p. 75 (1).

53. See TB, no. 16, p. 69 (5).

54. See TB, no. 17, p. 70 (3).

55. See TB, no. 17, p. 71 (5).

56. See Karol Wojtyla, *Love and Responsibility,* trans. H.T. Willetts (San Francisco: Ignatius Press, 1993), p. 41.

57. See TB, no. 19, p. 77 (5).

58. See TB, no. 20, p.79 (4).

59. See Genesis 4:1.

60. See TB, no. 22, p. 83 (3).

61. See TB, no. 22, pp. 85–86 (7).

62. See *The Roman Missal: The Sacramentary,* promulgated by Pope Paul VI on April 3, 1969, and trans. by the International Commission on English in the Liturgy (New York: Catholic Book Publishing, 1974), p. 843.

63. See TB, no. 22, p. 86 (7).

64. See TB, no. 23, pp. 88–89 (4).

The Human Person
after Sin

General Audience Addresses 24 to 63

A. Introduction: Addresses 24 to 25

The first cycle of the theology of the body began with a "word" of Christ regarding divorce—"beginning"—and led to a phenomenological analysis of the human being as an embodied person in the garden of Eden before sin. The second cycle also begins with the words of Christ, this time about adultery and lust. In the Sermon on the Mount, Christ taught the sixth commandment: "You have heard that it was said, 'You shall not commit adultery.'" But he added, "But I say to you, everyone who looks at a woman with lust has already committed adultery with her in his heart."[1]

Like Christ's reference to the "beginning," John Paul argues, this passage from the Sermon on the Mount is key to understanding the meaning of the theology of the body. It is significant both because of its "global context, through which the key meaning of the theology of the body will be revealed to us," and also because, in this teaching, "Christ fundamentally revises the way of understanding and carrying out the moral law of the old covenant."[2]

1. Christ Speaks to Us Today

As the pope explains, Christ's teaching on adultery is global in context because it is not intended merely for the particular audience that heard the Sermon on the Mount, but rather is a "general truth" that applies as much to all of us today as it did to the people of his own time. John Paul writes, Christ is addressing "historical man, . . . the man of a given moment of history and, at the same time, all men belonging to the same human history."[3] And not just "man," but also woman, for "The fact that Christ directly addresses man as the one 'who looks at a woman lustfully,' does not mean that his words, in their ethical meaning, do not refer also to woman."[4] Thus, everything he said and did speaks to all people of every age, every gender, every race, and every tongue, "both in the immense space of the past, and in the equally vast one of the future." Moreover, since all people have the common inheritance of the experiences of solitude, unity, and nakedness, Christ is speaking to people who know in the depths of their own hearts the meaning of human personhood—that is, that the body is the expression of the human person—and the nuptial meaning of the body.

2. Looking Lustfully

We are tempted to look lustfully because of sin. Therefore, to understand Christ's meanings in his teaching on adultery, it is necessary to examine the origins of sin in the sin of our first parents. Their sin is part of the common inheritance of the human race, shared by all except Christ and the Blessed Virgin. Thus, while the first word of Christ pointed to the way we were created without sin, the second word points to the way we are now—what the pope calls "historical man," the man affected by sin. He will undertake his analysis by reference specifically to Adam and Eve's experience of nakedness without original innocence. The teaching of Christ on adultery will offer the pope an opportunity to analyze the relationship of the human person to his or her body after original sin.

In address 24 we learn that Christ's teaching about adultery in the Sermon on the Mount is addressed to every single human being and is markedly different from the understanding of adultery in the Old Testament. Christ isn't interested just in the externals of an act, in what is done, but, much more important, in the interior dispositions of mind and will that a person has before, during, and after entering into a particular act. Christ is concerned not only with the action but also with the knowledge and intention that lie behind it. The pope writes, "Christ shifts the essence of the problem [of adultery] to 'another dimension' by saying, 'Everyone who looks at a woman lustfully has already committed adultery with her in his heart.'" (John Paul adds: "According to ancient translations, the text is: 'has already made her an adultress in his heart,' a formula which seems to be more exact.") "In this way," John Paul points out, "Christ appeals to the interior man."[5] Since Christ is talking about an internal act—looking lustfully—he is referring to what goes on inside the human person.

John Paul observes that Christ is seeking here to establish the true, interior meaning of the commandment "You shall not commit adultery" against interpretations that viewed the command in a merely external way. It is important, the pope says, to point out "the dimension of the interior action, referred to also in the words: 'You shall not commit adultery.'"[6] Unfortunately, a certain "casuistry" entered into discussion of this commandment in the Old Testament. Christ criticizes this later legislation for dealing with this commandment "according to exterior criteria," because "in this way, . . . the meaning of the commandment as willed by the legislator underwent a distortion."[7] Against this external view of the commandment, John Paul declares, "it is a question here of adhering to the meaning that God the legislator enclosed in the commandment, 'You shall not commit adultery.'"[8]

Christ wishes to focus on the interior dispositions of a person's mind and heart, or will, on the subjective, "interior perception of values."[9] Christ's emphasis on the interior disposition implies that the truths of morality and ethics must be internalized, that is, made part of us. Of course, this is precisely the major difficulty today in a culture that proclaims over and over again, "That may be true for you, but not for me." The pope's point is that followers of Christ must internalize the ethics and morality he taught, otherwise they simply are not followers of Christ! Being a follower of Christ does have a subjective dimension: we are called to perceive within our own experience the truth about who we are and to interiorize it in our mind and will. However, the truth that we are to perceive and interiorize exists objectively; it is not something that we produce ourselves. The truth about ourselves does not originate in us or vary from individual to individual. It has an objective existence. It does not originate in us but in God.

B. SATAN'S LIES: ADDRESS 26

While Christ's words in the Sermon on the Mount refer explicitly to feelings of lust in the human heart, John Paul points out that they also indirectly "guide us to understanding a truth about man, which is of universal importance."[10] This truth, he says, is expressed in the passage at 1 John 2:16-17 on the three forms of lust: "The lust of the flesh and the lust of the eyes and the pride of life, is not of the Father but is of the world."[11] Since lust is "of the world" and "not of the Father," the pope explains, the tendency to look lustfully comes not from humanity in its original state but from humanity wounded by sin. "The 'world' of Genesis has become the 'world' of the Johannine words (cf. John 2:15-16), the place and source of lust, only as a consequence of sin, as the fruit of the breaking of the covenant with God in the human heart, in the inner recesses of man."[12]

This point is essential because some would excuse lustful behavior as simply human. We have all heard it said, "We're only human after all," as an excuse for sin. But it is *fallen* human nature that we are talking about, not our nature as we were originally created. Such remarks are made to excuse not only sinful acts, but the sinful origin of these tendencies. Since we are created in God's image, we are, of necessity, of God. To regard ourselves as simply belonging to the world—to the world that is the result of sin—is to abandon any hope of living as we should. Lust is the result of sin. Sin and its effects must be fought with the help of God's grace.

Following the reference to St. John, the pope notes that since lust is the result of sin, it "seems to direct us once more to the biblical beginning,"[13] that is, to the origins of sin. The pope wishes to return to the early chapters of Genesis not to examine the state of man before sin but rather to examine the "breaking of the first covenant with the Creator."[14]

When the devil tempted her to eat the fruit of the forbidden tree, Eve countered, "If we eat this fruit, we shall surely die." To that, the devil replied, "You will not die! For God knows that when you eat of it your eyes will be opened, and you will be like God, knowing good and evil."[15] This famous line, which led to the catastrophic fall of man, actually contains three lies, which are essential for understanding the "breaking of the covenant" with God and, therefore, for understanding everything that follows in the theology of the body.

1. Satan's First Lie in the Garden of Eden

Satan casts doubt on God by asking Eve whether God had forbidden her and Adam to eat of any of the fruit of the trees of paradise. Eve responds that only one tree contains "forbidden fruit." She adds, "If we eat this fruit we shall surely die," and the devil responds: "You shall not die." Of course, in this line, Satan is calling God a liar, because it was God who had said that anyone who ate the forbidden fruit would die. Eve was faced with a dilemma: to regard either God as a liar or the devil as a liar. Tragically, Eve, and later Adam, believed the devil. Thus they accepted the first lie: that God is a liar. The acceptance of this lie clouded the human intellect, because in believing that God is a liar there is a direct rejection of the fundamental truth that God *is* truth. Since the human intellect is created to know the truth, the rejection of Truth itself wounded it in all the descendants of Adam and Eve (except Mary and Christ).

2. Satan's Second Lie in the Garden of Eden

The devil continues with the second lie: "No, God knows well that the moment you eat of it your eyes will be opened and you will be like God, knowing good and evil." Satan is promising Adam and Eve that they will be "like God." Now, this sounds as though they will be "like God" in the sense that they are created in God's image and likeness. But this is not at all what the devil means. If one believes the devil's first lie, God must be a liar. Who, then, would want to be like *him*? In fact, the devil is making *himself* out to be God. After all, if God is a liar, who else was around to take his place except the devil? This conclusion is partially dependent on the parallels between the devil's temptations of Eve and his temptations of Christ. The second lie, "You will be like God," parallels the temptation presented to Christ, "Fall down and worship me," that is, treat me as God.[16]

The acceptance of this lie wounded the human will, because the power to love is rooted in the will. In refusing to love God, who *is* love, and by attempting to love Satan, Adam and Eve rejected Love itself. Rejecting

Love itself wounded their power to love, their wills. With our inheritance of original sin from our first parents, the wills of all the descendants of Adam and Eve (except Mary and Christ) are darkened.

3. Satan's Third Lie in the Garden of Eden

The devil's third lie comes in the last phrase. The devil promises Adam and Eve that they will know what is good and evil, or, in a different translation, what is good and bad. This does not mean simply "knowing," but rather, creating good and evil. The devil is promising Adam and Eve not just that they will be "like God," but that they will be God *establishing* creation. According to this lie, they will have the power of creating the world in their own image.

In accepting this lie, Adam and Eve wounded their bodies, because they were attempting to be gods so they could fulfill every bodily desire. But the emotions and sensual powers of the human body were intended to be governed by the human mind and will. Adam and Eve disturbed this order, thus wounding their bodies—and passing this wound on to all their descendants, who suffer from the effects of original sin (again with the exception of Christ and his mother).

Of course, there is a contradiction between the second lie, in which the devil poses as God and invites Adam and Eve to become his followers, and the third lie, in which the devil offers Adam and Eve the opportunity to become gods. But this contradiction did not bother the devil. He was only trying to tempt Adam and Eve. We should realize that they had a very short time to consider what the devil was proposing, so we should not be too hard on our first parents. We have had centuries to consider the temptations and lies of the devil; they had seconds! Unfortunately, they assented to the temptation and took the forbidden fruit.

4. Adam and Eve's Motive in Accepting Satan's Lies

It was not the fruit itself that broke Adam and Eve's covenant with God. The problem was the rejection of God that eating the fruit symbolized, as well as their acceptance of the devil as god and their desire to be gods themselves. Even more troubling is their motive. Underneath the three lies of the devil is an insidious and literally diabolical motive. The devil makes the loving Father, the author of creation, into a cruel tyrant. In effect, he says: "You are created in God's image and likeness. You can fulfill yourselves by becoming more and more like God. The fruit of the tree which God told you not to eat will actually make you more like God. This fruit will help you fulfill yourselves as images of God. God told you not to eat this fruit because he does not want you to fulfill yourselves by becoming like him. He created you in his image, gave you a tree that would help you fulfill yourselves by becoming more like him, and then told you not to eat of it." The devil makes the loving Father into someone who enjoys taunting Adam and Eve. They could fulfill themselves—but God does not allow it. An apt comparison would be that of a man dying of thirst who is offered a glass of cold water, only to have it dashed out of his hands before he can take the first sip. By accepting this motive, Adam and Eve accepted God as a sadistic tyrant who did not love them but only wanted to torture them. The motive destroyed any trust that might have existed between God, on the one hand, and Adam and Eve, on the other. The pope summarizes all this when he writes, "This motivation clearly includes questioning the gift and the love from which creation has its origin as donation." John Paul makes the point even more clearly a little later in the same address: "Questioning in his heart the deepest meaning of the donation, that is, love as the specific motive of the creation and of the original covenant (cf. Genesis 3:5), man turns his back on God-Love, on the Father. In a way he casts God out of his heart."[17]

But human beings are created in God's image and likeness. An act against God is simultaneously an act against human beings themselves. In rejecting God, man rejects himself. In addition, since every act is contained in our consciousness, an act against God and ourselves, especially such a fundamental act as the first sin, wounds us irreparably. We become what we do. In the first sin, we became human beings who rejected God-Love and everything he did, including our own creation in his image. No wonder we needed a redeemer! We had seriously wounded ourselves.

C. Nakedness after Sin: Address 27

Adam and Eve experienced a change in themselves as a result of their sin. Before they sinned, they were naked but not ashamed.[18] After they sinned, "The eyes of both were opened, and they knew that they were naked; and they sewed fig leaves together and made themselves aprons."[19] Adam and Eve sinned and experienced shame. This shame registered in their consciousness and is recorded in the pages of Genesis. However, the pope writes, "We realize that something deeper than physical shame, bound up with a recent consciousness of his own nakedness, is in action here."[20] With Adam and Eve's experience of nakedness after sin, their awareness of their own bodies was radically different than it had been before. This altered consciousness of their bodies testifies to a radical change in themselves. Adam and Eve's experience of shame is not merely shame at their physical nakedness; it is shame rooted in a deeper kind of nakedness—the nakedness of being deprived of their original sharing in God's holiness and love, which God had intended for them "from the beginning." "Nakedness does not have solely a literal meaning," John Paul says. "It does not refer only to the body. . . . Actually, through nakedness, man deprived of participation in the gift is manifested, man alienated from that love which had been the source of the original gift, the source of the fullness of the good intended for the creature."[21]

Before sin, writes the pope, nakedness represented "full acceptance of the body in all its human and therefore personal truth." The body was the means by which man was able to know himself as a person. "As the expression of the person, the body was the first sign of man's presence in the visible world. In that world, right from the beginning, man was able to distinguish himself, almost to be individualized—that is, confirm himself as a person—through his own body. . . . The words 'I was afraid, because I was naked, and I hid myself' (Genesis 3:10), witness to a radical change." These words "confirm the collapse of the original acceptance of the body as a sign of the person in the visible world."[22] The collapse consists in the break that has now occurred between the personal powers of mind and will, on the one hand, and the body, on the other.

The first sin not only caused a change within Adam and Eve, it changed their relationship with God. Before sin, there was an easy and familiar relationship with God. Adam receives God's command not to eat of the tree of knowledge of good and evil without protest or reaction.[23] After sin, their shame led them to hide from God because their sin made them fearful of God. Fear always accompanies shame—fear of discovery of the act of which one is ashamed.

Adam and Eve perceived a change within themselves, especially in their bodies.[24] They found that their relationship with God was now characterized by fear. And they experienced a different relationship with the visible world. Adam and Eve were constituted as persons with bodies and invited to subdue the earth. The words of Adam, "I was afraid, because I was naked, so I hid myself," express, the pope says, "the awareness of being defenseless. They express the sense of insecurity of his bodily structure before the processes of nature."[25] In other words, before sin, Adam and Eve were in charge of the world. As persons, they were not subject to the natural processes, but nature was subject to them. After sin, this original order was reversed. Adam and Eve's fear after sin was the natural reaction to their new situation: fear at what the processes of nature might do to them.

D. A Constitutive Break within the Human Person: Address 28

In one of his most famous lines, John Paul writes that through the words "I was naked, and I hid myself," a certain "constitutive break within the human person is revealed, which is almost a rupture of man's original spiritual and somatic unity. He realizes for the first time that his body has ceased drawing upon the power of the spirit, which raised him to the level of the image of God." Consequently, there is "a fundamental disquiet in all human existence."[26] This disquiet lies in man's awareness that he is no longer able to control his own body. Before sin, the body always responded to the dictates of reason and free will. Now, after sin, the human body no longer responds to what the mind knows or the will chooses. Before sin, man was autonomous and could act on the basis of knowledge and choice. Now, "the structure of self-mastery . . . is shaken to the very foundations in him. . . . It is as if he felt a specific break of the personal integrity of his own body, especially in what determines its sexuality."[27]

We all have experiences of this break in ourselves. We all know that we might decide to eat only a few potato chips, but then eat the whole bag—and say, "I changed my mind." What happened was that the desires of the body, stimulated by the food, pressed the mind and the will. Weakened as they are by original sin, the mind and the will gave in. We think to ourselves, "One more chip won't hurt me," and then choose in our wills to eat another one. We alter our choice—we change our minds—because of the press of the bodily desires on our minds and wills.

In his Letter to the Romans, St. Paul refers to our lack of self-mastery when he writes, "I see in my members another law at war with the law of my mind, taking me captive to the law of sin that dwells in my members."[28] By "the law of sin" Paul means our tendency to give way to sinful desires against our mind's better judgment and against the good resolutions of our will. Before they sinned, Adam and Eve didn't experience this tendency to be overwhelmed by their desires. They enjoyed a mastery of themselves. Their minds and wills always orchestrated their bodily powers, not the other way around.

E. What the Constitutive Break Did to Adam and Eve's Relationship: Address 29

John Paul now analyzes what lust did to the communion of Adam and Eve. In original unity before sin, Adam and Eve each expressed through their bodies a total self-donation to the other. They gave themselves freely and without reservation, almost without thinking about it, with nothing held back and nothing taken from the other. After sin, lust caused them to see each other as purely sexual objects. They saw in each other the chance to benefit from the other through sexual pleasure. The "original capacity of communicating themselves to each other . . . has been shattered" by lust.[29] The sexual differences between Adam and Eve became "an element of mutual confrontation of persons."[30]

No longer were Adam and Eve able to see the full truth of each other—the truth that the other human being is an infinite and unexpected gift in all of his or her powers and capabilities. Rather, each was reduced in the mind of the other to a single value—the sexual one. Lust of the body focuses on one aspect of the person: his or her sexuality and what she or he can do for me to satisfy my lustful desires. This reduction of the other person to what he or she is for me represents an impoverishment of the other and results in a severe limitation of the communion of persons. Both Adam and Eve focused only on the sexuality of the other, and this new attitude undermined their relationship in two ways. First, the one lusting was not giving himself or herself but was only interested in taking from the other. Second, the one lusting saw only one aspect of the person—his or her sexuality—and missed the true value of the person as an unrepeatable and unique being created by God for his or her own sake. "It is as if the body, in its masculinity and femininity, no longer constituted the trustworthy substratum of the communion of persons." It was the original function of masculinity and femininity to express the person and communicate love. But now this original function is "called in question in the consciousness of man and woman."[31]

It is important to note the pope's claim that it is in the *consciousness* of Adam and Eve that the constitutive break within themselves is known. The experience of lust led Adam and Eve to the self-awareness that their bodies are now different, that their bodies speak a different and inappropriate language, that is, inappropriate to human dignity. This new self-awareness changes their appreciation of their own bodies and in turn changes the way they relate to one another in and through their bodies. Before sin, they were aware that their bodies were created as masculine and feminine so that they could give themselves to each other. After sin, they saw their physical differences not as a sign and means for their mutual self-donation to one another but rather as something each could take from the other. Since no one wishes to be taken, the new attitude of Adam and Eve toward the other's body led to an opposition, a confrontation between them. The pope goes so far as to say that the sexual differences between Adam and Eve now became an "obstacle" in the personal relationship between man and woman.[32]

Still, even after sin, Adam and Eve retained some knowledge of their own dignity and value. They knew that they were not mere things to be taken by another. To be perceived as a thing to be taken caused shame and reduced the trust between them. As the pope writes, "Hence the necessity of hiding before the other with one's own body, with what determines one's own femininity-masculinity. This necessity proves the fundamental lack of trust, which in itself indicates the collapse of the original relationship of communion."[33]

John Paul derives these conclusions from the words of Adam that he was afraid because he was naked, and so he hid himself. The words reveal shame and fear. The shame is present, on the surface, because of lust. But the pope argues that the lust itself points to a deeper problem: the "constitutive break within the human person." The implicit argument is that if Adam was ashamed, he was acting against his own value system.

We feel shame when we do something that we *know* we should not do. In other words, the feeling of shame serves as a sign to us that we have violated one of our values. "You should be ashamed of yourself" is the admonition of parents and guardians, advisors and counselors, when we have done something we should not have done. The remark is intended to reenkindle the value system which would hold us from doing that particular act. Seeing each other naked, after sin, Adam and Eve reacted in a way predictable to all of us. They experienced shame because their bodies expressed a sexual desire for one another that was contrary to their system of values. If Adam is ashamed of his lust, he holds a value system in which lust is wrong. So, why would he look lustfully at Eve? He does it because, as the pope points out, it is difficult for him not to do it. He cannot control his own body as he should. There is a constitutive break within him. Since this situation is contrary to the way he should be, the way he was created, he is ashamed, not so much of lust itself but of the break within himself—a break that, of course, he caused through his sin.

Nevertheless, by alerting us to the fact that we are acting against our values, the feeling of shame can actually help us control our behavior. If I believe I should tell the truth—that is, if I value truth—then I will feel ashamed of myself for lying. But shame does more than just tell me that I've done something wrong—it also helps me keep from violating that value in the future. For, once I *know* that I will feel ashamed if I act in a certain way, chances are that I will try not to act that way. The pope explains, "Shame has a double meaning. It indicates the threat to the value and at the same time preserves this value interiorly. The human heart, from the moment when the lust of the body was born in it, also keeps shame within itself."[34]

Since shame at lust indicates that lust violates one of our values, it is apparent that those who feel this shame—Adam and Eve and all of us "historical" men and women, who are wounded by original sin—still hold the value of true love, of true self-gift. That value, remaining within each of us, can be the object of an appeal, that is, the appeal Christ makes to all of us not to give in to lust. The pope explains, "This fact indicates that it is possible and necessary to appeal to the heart when it is a question of guaranteeing those values from which lust takes away their original and full dimension. If we keep that in mind, we can understand better why Christ, speaking of lust, appeals to the human 'heart.'"[35]

John Paul insists that all of us retain the self-knowledge gleaned from the original experiences of solitude, original unity, and nakedness with original innocence. These experiences form the core values that all descendants of Adam and Eve can come to know. However, the experience of nakedness without original innocence is also a common inheritance. The self-awareness of nakedness after sin also leads to a knowledge of ourselves. The true value system from the original experiences is in conflict with the false value system of the experience of nakedness without original innocence. The conflict between the original self-knowledge before sin and the self-knowledge gleaned after sin causes shame.

F. Lust and the Nuptial Meaning of the Body: Addresses 30 to 33

1. Insatiable Desire and Domination

In address 30 John Paul analyzes Genesis 3:16, in which God says to Eve, "Your urge shall be for your husband, and he shall be your master." In this statement, John Paul II sees the particular damage done to the communion between Adam and Eve in paradise before sin. "These words mean above all, a violation, a fundamental loss, of the original community-communion of persons."[36] Their union has been altered by sin. Because of lust, there is now an insatiable desire for the sexual union. In fact, as the pope writes, their union is even "threatened by the insatiability of that union."[37]

In address 31 we read that Adam and Eve are aware of what their communion should be and realize that they can no longer achieve such a union and rest in the happiness of their mutual gift to one another. The changed nature of their union is another cause of shame. They feel ashamed that they are unable to establish a nuptial communion of persons as God had intended from the beginning. This shame is in addition to their shame at the constitutive break within themselves.

Adam's shame and lust lead him to "dominate" the woman Eve.[38] The mechanism here is that Adam feels in his body a strong, lustful attraction to Eve—a desire to take rather than to give himself through his sexuality. This feeling of lust doesn't come gradually to Adam, as it does to most of us when we begin puberty, but comes suddenly as a result of original sin. Overwhelming lust bursts onto both Adam and Eve more or less out of the blue, and, never having experienced such lust before, they don't know how to handle it. At the same time, Adam feels shame at not establishing the nuptial communion of persons with Eve that God had intended them to enjoy. The combination of lust and shame leads him to attempt a union. We could imagine him thinking to himself, "Maybe if I try to unite with her, we can achieve something," and further, "If I unite with her, I will be able to satisfy these terrible longings." The result is that he dominates her.

Eve, for her part, also experiences lust. And she feels shame at not uniting with Adam in the full communion of persons as God had intended. She desires both to experience the full communion of persons and to satisfy her lustful longings. The pope says that she experiences an "insatiable desire for a different union."[39] He seems to mean that the experience of lust in women, combined with their experience of domination by husbands, leads them to look for other unions, that is, for other men, who would not dominate them and who could satisfy their strong feelings of attraction to the opposite sex. But obviously, the pope doesn't mean that only women are tempted to cheat on their marriages!

2. Men and Women Are Not Mere Things

"From the moment when the man 'dominates' her, the communion of persons . . . is followed by a different mutual relationship. This is the relationship of possession of the other as the object of one's own desire."[40] Instead of receiving the other as a gift and giving oneself in return, in a constantly recurring mutual giving and receiving, Adam and Eve now strive to own and possess one another. Clearly, this involves a using of the object owned and possessed. If I own a car, I can use it by driving it anywhere I choose. Similarly, if a woman is mine in the sense of ownership, I have the right to use her as an object. If one wants the source of the modern sexual revolution, this is it! Underlying every form of sexual sin that is approved of in contemporary culture is the view that our own sexual powers belong to us for our own enjoyment and that other people's sexual powers are also things we can own.

3. Lust as a Threat to Marriage

In address 32 the pope remarks that sexuality before sin "fully expressed the call of man and woman to personal communion. After sin, on the contrary, in the new situation of which Genesis 3 speaks, this expression was weakened and dimmed. It is as if it were . . . driven back to another plane."[41] Here, the other plane is purely physical and nonpersonal. "The human body in its masculinity and femininity has almost lost the capacity of expressing this love." However, "the nuptial meaning of the body has not been completely suffocated by concupiscence, but only habitually threatened."[42] The pope drives his point home with a line that expresses graphically, conclusively, and succinctly a major point of his entire theology of the body: "The heart has become a battlefield between love and lust."[43]

In other words, Adam and Eve and their descendants (except for Mary and Christ) now no longer clearly perceive that their bodies were created to be gifts for each other—that the body expresses the truth that human persons were created for love. Yet, although we have inherited original sin and its effects, the original nuptial meaning of the body has not been completely obliterated. Some semblance of this original meaning is still present in all of us.

Lust interferes with love, because it inhibits the freedom necessary to love. If a person is compelled by the desires of the flesh, that is, by lust, toward a physical union with another person, even his or her spouse, this is hardly love, because love is a completely free self-donation, chosen by the person in his or her *free* will. "Concupiscence entails the loss of the interior freedom of the gift. The nuptial meaning of the human body is connected precisely with this freedom."[44] Love is still possible if a person can freely choose to make a self-donation to the one loved. But this requires self-control, self-mastery, which is difficult. It is precisely this self-mastery that Christ had in mind in his comments regarding lust.

When we win the war between lust and love within ourselves, we come close to establishing a true loving communion of persons in the sense sketched in Genesis before Adam and Eve sinned. When we lose this war, our bodies no longer express a loving gift but actually convey to the other a wish to possess him or her. When we lose the battle between love and lust, "the subjectivity of the person gives way to the objectivity of the body. Owing to the body, man becomes an object for man—the female for the male and vice versa. . . . The relationship of the gift is changed into the relationship of appropriation."[45]

In the next address (33), the pope discusses the meaning of the word "my" in a loving nuptial union. He shows that in a loving union, the word "my" is applied to the spouse not as though the spouse were owned as a thing is owned but rather in an analogous sense. The two terms in an analogy have some similarities, but they also have dissimilarities. The analogy of a clover leaf to the Trinity is a case in point. In the clover leaf, there are three leaves in the one leaf, which is similar to the three Persons in the one Godhead. But there are obviously profound and fundamental dissimilarities between a clover and God. Clearly, when spouses use the word "my" in relationship to each other—"my husband" or "my wife"—there is both a similarity to possession or ownership but also a profound dissimilarity.

Although John Paul reiterates that husband and wife share mutual responsibility to maintain "the balance of the gift" to one another in the nuptial communion of persons, he does sees a subtle difference in the nature of their responsibility. Adam is sketched by the author of Genesis as the one who originally receives the gift.[46] After sin, he is the one who is tempted to dominate the woman. Although he notes that part of the differentiation in man's and woman's roles in Genesis was "dictated by the social emargination of woman in the conditions of that time," he nevertheless believes that "a special responsibility rests with man above all, as if it depended more on him whether the balance is maintained or broken or even—if already broken—reestablished."[47] From this point of view, the husband sets the tone in the nuptial communion of persons, even though, as John Paul reiterates, it is a mutual responsibility.

The best way of expressing this truth probably would be that, when the proper balance in marriage is lost, it is harder for the wife to reestablish it than for the husband; but, if she chooses, she can make it impossible for him to restore the balance. Further, it is harder for her to cause an imbalance in the relationship than it is for her husband; but she can, with difficulty, prevent him from maintaining the proper balance.

G. Introduction to Addresses 35 to 43: Address 34

The pope returns in addresses 34–43 to an analysis of the second word of Christ on marriage. He again quotes Christ's teaching from the Sermon on the Mount, "You have heard that it was said, 'You shall not commit adultery.' But I say to you, that every one who looks at a woman lustfully has already committed adultery with her in his heart."[48] John Paul then analyzes what the hearers of Christ would have understood by "adultery" (addresses 35 to 37), "looking lustfully" (addresses 38 to 41), and "adultery in the heart" (addresses 42 to 43).

In the introduction to these analyses (address 34), John Paul repeats a point he made toward the beginning of the second cycle.[49] In the Sermon on the Mount, Christ subjects legal forms to a critique and rejects a legalistic approach to the commandment against adultery by discussing various commandments and interpreting them according to the original intent of his Father: "You have heard it said, but I say to you. . . ." The commandments must be internalized and become part of the disposition of the heart. The content of the interiorization is a "new ethos, the ethos of the Gospel."[50] By this the pope means that the values taught since creation are not sufficient if they are exterior, but must be interiorized according to the original intent of the Creator as taught by Christ. For example, adultery can be committed not only by a wife; a husband can also commit adultery, by taking someone who is not his wife. The work of interiorization is difficult because of the hardness of heart in each of us caused by the wounds of sin.

The pope repeats his point that Christ can appeal to the human heart because Christ knows what is in man.[51] Christ could not reveal who we are and how we should act unless he knew us. But indeed, he knows us intimately. As God, he created each of us as an image of God. As the God-man, he reveals to all of us what it means to be an image of God. Therefore, in the Sermon on the Mount, Christ is speaking not just to those who heard him in Palestine two thousand years ago but to each and every one of us. And, as the pope argues, we all feel "called, in an adequate, concrete and unrepeatable way."[52] That is, each of us is called in our own situation, according to our own individuality, and in a way that is entirely appropriate for us as an individual. When Christ calls us to recognize the lust in our hearts, this is not an accusation but a true call. Christ is stating what is truly in man and then issuing a call to overcome the wounds of sin. "Christ appeals to the human heart."[53]

H. Adultery: Addresses 35 to 37

In address 35 John Paul sketches the situation of the audience who heard Christ speak about adultery. He traces the Old Testament tradition, which Christ's audience fully comprehended because they lived in a society formed by that tradition. He shows how, in the Old Testament, as a result of the hardness of heart caused by sin, a certain kind of interpretation developed that negated the content of God's commandment against adultery. Since procreation was essential for the chosen people, men were allowed to have more than one wife. Monogamy was abandoned. Originally, God may have allowed this exception so that more children could be born, but it was certainly continued by men for the sake of satisfying concupiscence, or lust. In the eyes of the Old Testament, polygamy was not a violation of the commandment against adultery. Adultery was primarily the taking of one man's wife by another man, for example, the taking of Uriah's wife, Bathsheba, by David.[54]

In order to allow polygamy while upholding the sixth commandment, "Thou shalt not commit adultery," adultery had to be defined through an exterior set of laws that excluded polygamy. The pope calls these laws "casuistic,"[55] meaning that they were merely external laws with little basis in the truth of revelation founded in Genesis. Christ was not interested in discussing the Old Testament external law code. He was interested in penetrating to the "full truth about man" and reshaping the consciences of his listeners and, through them, of all of us.

The next address (36) traces the external laws of the Old Testament in greater detail. John Paul shows that these external laws actually legalized sin by permitting polygamy. But homosexual behavior and bestiality were forbidden under pain of death. In effect, the Old Testament external laws tolerated polygamy for the sake of procreation (and did not call concupiscence into question) while forbidding other sexual activities that were not procreative. "The matrimonial law of the Old Testament, in its widest and fullest meaning, puts in the foreground the procreative end of marriage."[56] It prohibited sexual sin only partially, because it was only concerned with the external social order. As the pope writes, the laws of the Old Testament were "not concerned directly with putting some order in the heart of man, but with putting order in the entire social life, at the base of which stands, as always, marriage and family."[57] Christ, however, wanted to "restore in the conscience of his audience the ethical significance of this commandment"—that is, the commandment against adultery.[58]

In address 37 John Paul describes the vision of the Old Testament prophets with regard to marriage and adultery. In the prophetic books, in contrast to the law books, there is no "bow"—no expression of toleration—toward polygamy. Attempting to teach the people of Israel what idolatry was, the prophets compared God to a bridegroom and the people to his bride. In the prophets' application of marriage imagery to the relationship between God and Israel, a view of marriage was reflected that emphasized the "interpersonal structure of . . . love" and the "interior 'normativity' of the communion of the two people."[59] In this relationship, Israel should remain faithful, as any bride should; God was always faithful. In reality, through idolatry, the bride, the people of Israel, abandoned her husband, God; but God always called his bride back to him and forgave her. Obviously, this imagery relies on an entirely different view of the marriage covenant than the legal tradition of the Old Testament. But the people of the Old Testament were not aware of this obvious contradiction between the prophetic teaching and their external laws. Yet, John Paul observes, "By virtue of the prophetic tradition these listeners were in a certain sense prepared for adequately understanding the concept of adultery."[60]

I. Looking Lustfully: Addresses 38 to 41

In these four addresses, the pope examines what Christ meant, and what Christ's audience understood, by the words, "looking lustfully."

In address 38 John Paul essentially makes two points. The first is that Christ is announcing a new ethical norm. The judgment as to the rightness or wrongness of a human act must depend not just on what is done but also on the interior disposition of the mind and will of the one acting. The pope shows that Christ, in his remark about looking lustfully and committing adultery in the heart, shows that adultery can be committed without an exterior act of the body.

The second point the pope makes in this address is that those hearing Christ's remarks on adultery and looking lustfully were prepared for the new ethical norm Christ announced by some of the teachings in the Wisdom literature of the Old Testament, even though these texts never changed the "fundamental structure of ethical evaluation" of the Old Testament culture.[61] The Wisdom books, which are "distinguished for their special knowledge of the human heart," highlight the interior disposition of the human heart.[62]

In address 39, John Paul notes that Christ did not explain what "looking lustfully" meant. In fact, even fictional works and the Old Testament describe this act in much more detail than Christ did. But Christ did not need to explain himself further, because everyone who heard him probably knew what he meant from his or her own experience. Concupiscence, or lust, is like a fire manifested in and through the body that consumes the one lusting, because it is almost never satisfied. In talking about the lustful look, Christ "wanted to bring out that the man looks in conformity with what he is: *intueri sequitur esse* [the looking follows on his being]. In a certain sense, man by his look reveals himself to the outside and to others. Above all he reveals what he perceives on the 'inside.'"[63] This is another way of stating one of the central themes of the theology of the body: the body is the expression of the person, that is, of the person's thoughts and attitudes.

The final point of address 39 anticipates the major theme of the next address: in the lustful look, the nuptial significance of the body ceases to exist for the one lusting. All human beings respond to values, that is, to things that attract us. In the lustful look, the one looking is attracted by a certain value, that is, the sexual value of the other person. But perceiving the masculine or feminine as having only a sexual value is a terrible reduction, a diminishing of the meaning of the other person. Every person, while retaining his masculinity or her femininity, which includes the sexual value, or attractiveness, is of infinite value and worth, with an entire range of attractive characteristics and features. The one who reduces another simply to his or her sexual value is like a man whose friend is an auto mechanic. On one particular day, because his car needs repair, he brings the car to his friend and, without greeting him or treating him as a friend, simply expects him to fix his car inexpensively. The first man almost eliminates the other as a friend by reducing all of the qualities that have made him a friend to one, single value that is currently attractive; that is, his mechanical ability.

Lust obscures "the pyramid of values that marks the perennial attraction of male and female."[64] Thus, lust not only reduces a person to one value, that is, masculinity or femininity; it even ignores other values associated with masculinity and femininity, such as the charm of the feminine, the courage of the masculine, or the possibility of giving new life. "Lust has the internal effect, that is, in the heart, on the interior horizon of man and woman, of obscuring the significance of the body, of the person itself. Femininity . . . ceases bearing in itself the wonderful matrimonial significance of the body."[65] It ceases, that is, not in reality, in the woman, but in the mind of the man who looks with lust. All this happens with the look, because the look changes the way the other exists for the one looking. The pope summarizes his point in the last lines of address 40. Through lust, the woman "begins to be only an object of carnal concupiscence. To that is connected the profound inner separation of the matrimonial significance of the body."[66]

The point of address 41 is that the lustful look changes the way the two people exist. Created to be a mutual "for" in love through the communion of persons, an imitation of the Trinity, they now exist as objects of use. Both are reduced to objects in each other's eyes. The one who looks lustfully reduces the other to a thing, and since they share the same humanity, the one who looks lustfully also is reduced to the level of a thing. Of course, for this change to occur completely requires the one looking lustfully to choose in his or her will to look this way and also to realize in his or her intellect what is happening. If there is a consent of the will with knowledge of what is happening, the lustful look calls into question "the man's and the woman's way of existing as persons, . . . in a mutual 'for,' which . . . can and must serve the building up of the unity of communion in their mutual relations."[67] Once there is consent in the will with a knowledge of what is happening, the one looking lustfully has determined himself or herself, that is, has shaped himself or herself into a different sort of existence, because the lustful look is contained within his or her consciousness. With this shaping, they perceive themselves differently; their mutual "meaning" has changed. The one looking lustfully has wounded his or her humanity and even changed the way the other exists—at least in the mind of the one looking.

J. Adultery in the Heart: Addresses 42 to 43

In address 42 the pope asks how adultery, an act of the body in which a man and a woman who are not legally married to each other unite so as to become one flesh, can be committed only within a person, in the heart. The answer is that the adultery is in the interior disposition of the one who looks at the other in a selfish way (the biblical example speaks about a man looking at a woman, although it is certainly possible for a woman to look at a man in a similar way). The interior disposition revealed in the lustful look views the other as "someone for me" rather than "someone to whom I can give myself." This point echoes what the pope first taught in his book, *Love and Responsibility*, as "the personalistic norm": "The person is the kind of good which does not admit of use and cannot be treated as an object of use and as such the means to an end. . . . The person is a good toward which the only proper and adequate attitude is love."[68] "Love" is the gift of oneself to another and the receiving of the other's gift of self in return. "Use" is seeing in the other person something that that person can do for me. Lust is use. A lustful look expresses the interior disposition of the one looking, and this interior disposition views the other as a someone who can do something for the one looking; the interior disposition of the one looking reduces the other to an object of use. In this way, lust is adultery in the heart.

As the pope states in address 43, Christ makes the "moral evaluation of the desire depend above all on the personal dignity itself of the man and the woman."[69] In other words, adultery in the heart does not depend on sexual intercourse between a spouse and someone of the opposite sex to whom he or she is not in a marital relationship, but rather on a violation of the dignity and value of the two people. Their dignity and value require that they not be reduced to objects of use either by themselves or by the other. When they are so reduced, even in the mind of another, their dignity is attacked. Thus, adultery in the heart occurs when we view another as an object to be used for sexual pleasure.

At the end of address 42 the pope asks a question that he deals with in address 43: If reducing another to an object of use through lust is adultery in the heart, and adultery can only be committed by a married person uniting with someone who is not his or her spouse, then is adultery in the heart possible between spouses? The pope first presents the argument that a married couple *cannot* commit adultery in the heart, because adultery can only be committed by a spouse uniting in a marital way with someone of the opposite sex who is not his or her husband or wife. But then he shows the deficiency of this line of reasoning. If adultery in the heart depends on the way one is interiorly disposed toward another person, then certainly it is possible for a husband or a wife to commit adultery in the heart toward his or her spouse! Looking at the relationship from the viewpoint of the husband, the pope says that looking lustfully at his wife "changes the very intentionality of the woman's existence 'for' man. It reduces the riches of the perennial call to the communion of persons, the riches of the deep attractiveness of masculinity and femininity, to mere satisfaction of the sexual need of the body. . . . A man who looks in this way, as Matthew 5:27-28 indicates, uses the woman, her femininity, to satisfy his own instinct. . . . Man can commit this adultery in the heart also with regard to his own wife, if he treats her only as an object to satisfy instinct."[70] Obviously, this must be true if adultery in the heart consists of looking lustfully and reducing the existence of another to a being to be used.

Of course, this teaching is severe and requires of all of us a constant vigilance over our own hearts, most especially in marriage, because that union must be built on a profound appreciation of the dignity and value of the other. But, as John Paul assures us, we have the help of Christ through the redemption of the body, which, with regard to our interior dispositions toward other people, is conferred through "purity of heart." John Paul will spend many addresses on the question of purity of heart.

K. CHRIST APPEALS TO THE HUMAN HEART: ADDRESSES 44 TO 46

Christ's teaching on lust and adultery is rather stringent. He could be interpreted as accusing all historical men and women, that is, all men and women affected by original sin. The pope specifically asks this question: Is the heart accused by Christ's words?[71] The pope also asks what the person who accepts Christ's words should do. How should such a person act? How are Christ's words binding on the interior person, on the hearts of each of us, and how are these interior attitudes of the heart translated into appropriate action?

Since each of us is a completely free agent, we each act according to our own insights and values. Christ's words need to be interiorized. Each of us is called to accept them in our own conscience, to make them part of our own value system, and then we strive to act according to them. This is what John Paul II calls the process of the "interpenetration of ethos and praxis."[72] In other words, we interiorize the values Christ taught and then act in a way that follows this interiorization of his teachings. This process is for the most part private and hidden, but it goes on continually within the heart of each one of us as we enter into a dialogue with Christ and face various situations day by day.

At the same time, intellectuals have written about their reactions to Christ's words. They have made public their encounter and dialogue with Christ. The pope calls these reflections the "echo" of Christ's words.

1. The Error of Manichaeism

One such echo is the Manichaean interpretation, which held that it was not just lust that was condemned by Christ but the object of lust also, that is, the human body in its masculinity and femininity. In the Manichaean view, it is not the lustful look—and the attitude revealed in it—that is evil; the object of the lustful look is itself evil. The evil is transferred in the Manichaean view from the interior attitude to the object looked at. In this way, the Manichaean point of view throws the baby out with the bath water, because it condemns not just the sinful desire, that is, the lust; it also condemns the body through which the human person experiences the lust and the body at which the lust is directed. From this point of view, if a man lusts for a woman, the man's body through which he experiences the sinful desire is evil, and so is the woman's body. This kind of transference is common in many areas of human endeavor. For example, there are those who would say that guns are evil in themselves because they are used to kill people. This is an example of transferring the evil of an act from within a person to an exterior object. (This is not to deny that guns are dangerous and need to be properly controlled.)

In the Manichaean interpretation of Christ's words, it is the human body itself that is evil. As the pope writes, this is a terrible distortion of Christ's meaning. The Lord condemns the lust, but not the human body! The Manichaean viewpoint is even an attempt, the pope teaches, "to avoid the requirements set in the Gospel by him who 'knew what was in man' (John 2:25)."[73] The gospel calls each person to recognize the value of masculinity and femininity and live in the body in a way that aims at a true communion of persons. The Manichaean undercuts this effort by denying any meaning to the body.

In address 45 we read that Christ's words on adultery and adultery in the heart, far from being a condemnation of the body, are the affirmation of man's body "as an element which . . . shares in his dignity as a person."[74] A Manichaean attitude would lead to an "annihilation" of the body as an evil.[75] By contrast, Christ is appealing to all people to realize the immense value of the human body as the expression of the human person and as the means of expressing a profound personal union of love. "For the Manichaean mentality, the body and sexuality constitute an 'anti-value,'" while for Christianity "they always remain a value not sufficiently appreciated,"[76] because, in the pope's view, even Christianity has not yet fully appreciated the meaning of the human body.

The words of Christ in Matthew 5:27-28, far from lending themselves to a condemnation of the human body, "must lead to such an affirmation of the femininity and masculinity of the human being, as the personal dimension of 'being a body.'"[77] What the pope teaches here must be true, if we accept what he has taught in previous audiences. If Christ condemns lust because it is a reduction of the mystery of femininity and masculinity to the sexual value—a reduction that devalues and depersonalizes both the one who looks and the one who is the object of the look—then, obviously, Christ is aiming at reaffirming the full range of values of masculinity and femininity; that is, the full range of values associated with being a body. Far from a condemnation of the body, Christ's teaching reestablishes it with the full goodness of creation, the goodness that the Creator saw when he said that his work of creation on the sixth day, culminating in the creation of the embodied human person, was "very good."[78]

Toward the end of address 45, the pope remarks that not only are Christ's words not a condemnation of the body, they are not even a condemnation of the human heart. Rather, Christ is appealing to the human heart. He is asking each of us not to submit to the temptations of lust. "The appeal to master the lust of the flesh springs precisely from the affirmation of the personal dignity of the body and of sex, and serves only this dignity."[79]

2. Freud, Marx, and Nietzsche: Masters of Suspicion

In address 46 John Paul contrasts Christ's appeal with the condemnation of the human heart made by those he calls the "masters of suspicion": Freud, Marx, and Nietzsche. These three men, argues John Paul, probed the triple forms of lust mentioned in Scripture. Freud offered an analysis of the psychology of lust of the flesh. Flesh in this context and in its use by St. Paul usually connotes not the human body in all of its dignity, but rather the sinful desires of the body that strain against the sense of human dignity known by the intellect and embraced by the will. Marx presented a theoretical explanation for what the Bible calls the lust of the eyes—the lust for wealth and things. Nietzsche explored what the Bible calls the pride of life—the lust to make oneself into an all-powerful being. It is an excessive self-love that shuts out everyone else. Freud, Marx, and Nietzsche accused humanity of these forms of lust, but offered no solution, no way to overcome these weaknesses. Thus, we are left with the accusation and nothing else.

Christ also identifies these forms of lust, particularly the lust of the flesh. But he does not stop with the accusation. At the same time that he warns us not to look lustfully, he appeals to each of us to live in accordance with the original plan manifested so wondrously in Genesis before sin. He calls us to reaffirm the dignity of the human body in the marvelous differences of masculinity and femininity. Christ makes this appeal, and it is an effective one, because simultaneously with the appeal, Christ gives us the means of responding: the redemption and the grace flowing from it.

"Redemption is a truth, a reality, in the name of which man must feel called, and 'called with efficacy' . . . to rediscover, nay more, to realize the nuptial meaning of the body . . . to express in this way the interior freedom of the gift."[80]

"The appeal contained in Christ's words in the Sermon on the Mount cannot be an act detached from the context of concrete existence. It always means—though only in the dimension of the act to which it refers—the rediscovery of *the meaning of the whole of existence, of the meaning of life*, in which there is contained also that meaning of the body which here we call 'nuptial'" [emphasis added]. These words of Christ, John Paul continues, "reveal not only another ethos, but also another vision of man's possibilities. It is important that he, precisely in his heart, should not only feel irrevocably accused and given as prey to the lust of the flesh, but that he should feel forcefully called in this same heart. He is called precisely to that supreme value that is love. He is called as a person in the truth of his humanity, therefore also in the truth of his masculinity and femininity, in the truth of the body. He is called in that truth which has been his heritage from the beginning, the heritage of his heart, which is deeper than the sinfulness inherited, deeper than lust in its three forms. The words of Christ, set in the whole reality of creation and redemption, reactivate that deeper heritage and give it real power in man's life."[81]

L. The Relationship of Eros and Ethos: Addresses 47 to 49

Having established that Christ is appealing to the human heart—not condemning it because of lust, as the "masters of suspicion" had—the pope goes on to discuss the relationship of *eros*, that is, erotic love, with *ethos*, that is, ethical love. Of course, ethical love is the love that takes into account the entire human person, not just the sexual value. Erotic love usually is defined as the mutual attraction of masculine and feminine.

Erotic love is usually associated with lust. But, as the pope notes in address 47, *eros* as defined by Plato "represents the interior force that drags man toward everything good, true and beautiful."[82] If one considers the erotic love of masculine-feminine attraction in terms of Plato's definition, erotic love would be the attraction of one person to the entire value, the entire good, of the other person. In Plato's definition, erotic love would not merely be the attraction of the man to the feminine in the woman, to the sexual value of her as a woman, but rather his attraction to her whole being, to her, in all her personal worth and value. According to Plato's definition, in erotic love there would be no reduction of the other to merely his or her sexual value.

As erotic love is commonly used in literature and in modern parlance, it is the attraction of one to the other in terms of the other's sexual value. It represents, therefore, as the pope has mentioned previously in his examination of these matters, a reduction of the other to merely his or her sexual value. But, as the pope notes, in Plato's definition eros has room for ethos.[83] "In the erotic sphere, eros and ethos do not differ from each other. They are not opposed to each other, but are called to meet in the human heart, and, in this meeting, to bear fruit. What is worthy of the human heart is that the form of what is erotic should be at the same time the form of ethos, that is, of what is ethical."[84] The fruit of the meeting of eros and ethos is authentic love. In address 48 John Paul notes that if "the passion of the body" stops "at mere lust devoid of ethical value . . . then man, male and female, does not experience that fullness of eros, which means the aspiration of the human spirit toward what is true, good and beautiful."[85] In other words, if we are to discover the truth, goodness, and beauty of each person, we must always try to appreciate not just the sexual value of the other, but the whole person, in all her or his value and dignity.

We have all felt the tug of the desires of the flesh, of lust. We also have experienced the true gift of love to another person and the simultaneous gift of the other to us. This happens not just in marriage but also in friendship, in the relationships between brothers and sisters, between parents and children, and so on. The giving and receiving in a relationship of true love is far more satisfying then the momentary excitement of a rush of sensuality or emotion separated from authentic love—that is, lust. The gift of oneself and the receiving of the gift of another person in a true, loving relationship gives us a much deeper and much longer-lasting joy than the experience of mere sensuality. True eroticism—the attraction to the good, true, and beautiful—takes into account the whole person. Thus the form of true eros becomes the ethical norms laid down by Christ. As the pope writes, "When sexual desire is linked with a noble gratification, it differs from desire pure and simple. . . . Sexual excitement is very different from the deep emotion with which not only interior sensitivity, but sexuality itself reacts to the total expression of femininity and masculinity."[86] The pope is not saying that sensual excitement is to be rejected but that it is to be tied into the movement of love that draws spouses into a communion of persons. Spouses do not aim at mere sexual excitement but at "noble gratification"—the integration of emotion, sentiment, and sensual desire into true self-giving love.

1. Ethical Love Can Be Spontaneous

Some would argue that by requiring thought, ethical norms destroy a certain spontaneity. Spontaneity in the sense that people often think of it, that is, acting on mere sensuality or emotions, can lead one to enjoy the moment. In the view of some, acting ethically and resisting those sensual and emotional impulses squelches spontaneity and thus removes the possibility of enjoying the moment. But what do we gain from acting on bodily impulses "devoid" as they are "of an adequate hierarchy," that is, a recognition of true values?[87]

We gain nothing by that kind of spontaneity, since we are not acting as human persons should act, making choices on the basis of the dignity and value of ourselves and others. Instead, we reduce the other to a mere thing, and we become mere things ourselves. We end by reducing ourselves to nonpersons, even if that is not what we were intending. Of course, we remain persons, but in acting as though we were not persons, we wound ourselves and others. We also fail to discover the wonderful joy of giving and receiving love, because there is no love without an "adequate hierarchy" of values, that is, without acting on the basis of knowledge of our own dignity and that of the other.

If, however, there is a constant and consistent attitude within oneself of recognizing human dignity, then spontaneity on the basis of that attitude, which requires self-control, is not only good, but wonderful. If a husband and wife have achieved a certain self-control allowing them to have a constant attitude of appreciating human dignity, and on the spur of the moment, they wish to enter into the marital embrace, the lovemaking may be spontaneous, unplanned, but it will be based on an "adequate hierarchy" of values.

2. Ethical Love and Self-Control

"It is precisely at the price of self-control that man reaches that deeper and more mature spontaneity with which his heart, mastering his instincts, rediscovers the spiritual beauty of the sign constituted by the human body in its masculinity and femininity. . . . The human heart becomes a participant in another spontaneity, of which 'carnal man' knows nothing or very little."[88] In contrast to the false spontaneity that seeks mere sensual enjoyment, there is a true spontaneous love that involves the recognition of one's own dignity and that of the other. It involves an awareness of the nuptial meaning of the body and acts in accordance with that meaning. We each need to become what the pope calls "interior" persons so that we will always conform our external acts to the interior demands of our awareness of the nuptial meaning of the human body. We need to be like guardians watching over a hidden spring, discerning which moves of that spring are consistent with human dignity and the nuptial meaning of the body, and which are not. This process of discernment gradually becomes a consistent pattern in us. In time, it becomes almost second nature. Once this happens, there can be a true spontaneity, the result not just of passion and emotion but of an appreciation of human dignity and the nuptial meaning of the body.

The sexual attraction is greatly strengthened and deepened when it springs not just from passion and emotion but from "the total expression of femininity and masculinity."[89] This truth partially explains how couples, long married and aging, are more deeply in love than they were on the day of their marriage, even though others seeing such a couple may not understand how they could possibly by physically attracted to one another anymore. When our interior awareness and choices are in accordance with the nuptial meaning of the body, and this attitude becomes almost second nature, we become capable of a rich, spontaneous love that gives unbelievable joy and pleasure to ourselves and those we love. Of course, sometimes we sin. But through the help of Christ's grace, we can achieve a self-mastery that leads to the wonderful, loving spontaneity the pope is talking about.

3. Purity of Heart

Experiencing erotic love through ethical norms requires self-mastery, which is achieved through purity of heart. Speaking of the ethical norms laid down by Christ and made possible by him through the graces won for us through his cross and resurrection, John Paul says in address 49, "The ethos of redemption is realized in self-mastery, by means of temperance, that is, continence of desires."[90] Through self-mastery, we rediscover the capacity to perceive the nuptial meaning of the body—the truth that we are called to give ourselves in a loving self-surrender to God and others—and the capacity to relate to others in a way that accords with this meaning. Temperance, that is, the virtue of moderating our responses to pleasure, and continence, the virtue of controlling our responses to sexual desires, are achieved through purity of heart. The pope concludes the forty-ninth address with a statement that seems obvious after what he has just taught: "Purity is a requirement of love. It is the dimension of its interior truth in man's heart."[91]

M. PURITY LEADS TO FREEDOM: ADDRESSES 50 TO 53

Purity is a requirement of love, because it allows us to attain self-mastery— that is, it allows us to respond to others according to their true value and dignity as images of God. John Paul points out in address 50 that in the Old Testament the issue of spiritual purity—that is, of a human being's attitude with regard to other human beings, especially those of the opposite sex—was confused with cleanliness of the body. In the Old Testament "an erroneous way of understanding moral purity developed. It was often taken in the exclusively exterior and material sense."[92] John Paul shows that Christ clearly identifies purity with holiness and the opposite of purity with sin. "All moral good is a manifestation of purity, and all moral evil is a manifestation of impurity."[93] Citing St. Paul, the pope shows that purity is to be identified with life according to the Spirit, and impurity, with life according to the world or to the flesh.

1. Holiness as an Internal Disposition

John Paul relates St. Paul's discussion living in the flesh and living in the Spirit with Christ's teaching about purity and impurity. For both St. Paul and Christ, these concepts concern a person's fundamental disposition, his basic orientation, his inner and outer dimensions. Moreover, Christ and St. Paul use them to refer not only to sexual attitudes and behavior but to the entire range of moral attitudes and behavior.

In address 51, John Paul shows that "in the language of St. Paul's letters, the flesh indicates not only the 'exterior' man, but also the man who is 'interiorly' subjected to the 'world.'"[94] The pope shows that all of Paul's writings about the world and the flesh have this stamp. By the same token, life according to the Spirit, in other words, life with purity of heart, means for St. Paul not just an avoidance of sin but an interior attitude, an interior stance toward holiness. Just as sinfulness is not just a question of exterior actions but of internal dispositions, so also holiness is not just a question of exterior actions but of inner dispositions. John Paul clarifies what he means when he writes that with holiness "there is an effort of the will, the fruit of the human spirit permeated by the Spirit of God."[95]

This does not mean that the one who seeks to live according to the Spirit—who has a disposition toward holiness and makes an effort to resist temptation to sin—is sinless. There have been only two sinless human beings in history: Christ and his mother. Rather, the one who strives for holiness, who makes the effort in his or her will to resist temptation to sin, has intellectually accepted the demands of the gospel and strives in his or her will to overcome the temptations of the flesh, the world, and concupiscence in order to live according to those values. But this effort is almost certainly doomed to fail without the help of the Spirit, that is, without the help of God's grace. When such a person commits a sin, there is almost always a ready admission of the sin, sorrow, an expression of contrition to God, and a firm purpose of amendment and conversion. Such a person picks himself off the floor and begins again. This attitude contrasts with the person who may superficially admit that they did something "the church teaches is a sin" but is not truly contrite. Such a person has not internalized the value system of the gospel and does not have the constant disposition to try to live up to that value system.

The stark contrast between these two stances is readily apparent. When a priest hears the confession of someone with the first attitude, that is, one who has interiorly accepted the gospel values, there is very little work the priest needs to do as a spiritual counselor, because the penitent has already acknowledged his or her sin and asked forgiveness, and has a firm purpose of amendment. Such a penitent knows exactly what needs to be done. With a person with the second attitude, that is, one who has not interiorly accepted the gospel value system, the priest needs to try to persuade them of the gospel values in the first place. If convinced, the penitent can be led to a sorrow for the sin, repentance, and conversion. But unlike the case of the first penitent, such a stance is quite new, and such a person needs some weeks or months to fully accept the moral teachings of the gospel. It is clear that when John Paul talks about life according to the Spirit as an interior attitude, he does not mean that people who live according to the Spirit are sinless. He means that they strive toward holiness because they know what holiness as taught in the New Testament requires: the ethos of the redemption.

John Paul now moves on to discuss the range of meaning in the concepts of purity and impurity, of living according to the flesh and according to the Spirit. Christ uses purity to mean more than just the absence of sexual sins. Purity can mean the absence of all "dirt," of all sin; more deeply, it means the source of all moral good. In Matthew 15:18-19, Christ speaks of impurity as a defilement deep within the person when he says that "the things that come out of the mouth come from the heart, and they defile. For from the heart come evil thoughts, murder, adultery, unchastity, theft, false witness, blasphemy."[96] In a corresponding way, purity of heart results in the opposite of these acts: affirming the dignity of life, lifelong permanence and fidelity in marriage, chastity, respecting people's reputations and property, and affirming the one true God and not false gods.

St. Paul also uses purity in a general sense. He contrasts the flesh and the Spirit: "For the flesh has desires against the Spirit, and the Spirit against the flesh."[97] In the Pauline letters, flesh is opposed "not only and not so much to the human spirit as to the Holy Spirit who works in man's soul (spirit)."[98] The works of the flesh according to St. Paul are "immorality, impurity, licentiousness, idolatry, sorcery, hatreds, rivalry, jealousy, outbursts of fury, acts of selfishness, dissensions, factions, occasions of envy, drinking bouts, orgies, and the like."[99] On the other hand, "the fruit of the Spirit is love, joy, peace, patience, kindness, generosity, faithfulness, gentleness, self-control."[100] St. Paul's list of the sins of the flesh is very similar to Christ's list of sins that defile in Matthew 15:18-19. "The things that come out of the mouth come from the heart, and they defile. For from the heart come evil thoughts, murder, adultery, unchastity, theft, false witness, blasphemy."[101] All the works of the flesh defile, that is, they are opposed to purity. All the works of the spirit, that is, the Holy Spirit, are pure. Purity designates not only chastity and the absence of sexual sins but the absence of all sins that defile.

Purity is equated with life. "If you live according to the flesh, you will die, but if by the spirit you put to death the deeds of the body, you will live."[102] There is a contrast here between the death to the body and the moral death that results from sin. Death to the body, which involves dying to the desires of the flesh, leads to true life, life according to the Holy Spirit, life in the kingdom of God. Letting the desires of the body rule leads to true death, the death that denies us any participation in the kingdom of God.

Purity leads to self-mastery—which in turn gives us holiness—and holiness gives us freedom. Freedom is only present when there is the ability not only to say yes but also, when appropriate, to say no. Self-mastery gives us this possibility and in turn gives us holiness that is constituted by freedom: freedom from lust and from the desires of the body. The self-mastery attained through purity, which results in freedom, yields one set of actions from the heart, while the lack of that freedom caused by lack of self-mastery yields a different set of actions.

St. Paul contrasts purity, self-mastery, holiness, and freedom with defilement, lack of control, absence of holiness, and lack of freedom. Put in this fashion, the choice for all of us seems obvious.

2. The Opposition in Every Person between the Flesh and the Soul

Purity and self-mastery yield holiness and freedom. They are attained by the mind and will governing the body. However, it is very important to note that Christ and St. Paul are not suggesting that there is a fundamental separation between human flesh and the human soul imbedded in all human persons from the beginning—or even from the moment of the first sin. Andrew Marvell suggested in his wonderful poem "A Dialogue Between the Soul and Body" that the soul is enslaved by the flesh, and the body is ruled by a tyrannical soul. But, as the pope writes, "It is not a question here only of the body (matter) and of the spirit (the soul), as of two essentially different anthropological elements which constitute from the beginning the essence of man. But it presupposes that disposition of forces formed in man with original sin, in which every historical man participates. In this disposition, formed within man, the body opposes the spirit and easily prevails over it."[103] In other words, there is after sin a "constitutive break within the human person."[104] The clearest statement of this problem in Scripture is probably from the author of Romans: "I do not do the good I want, but I do the evil I do not want."[105]

But we can win this struggle within each of us through the power of the Holy Spirit. We can choose the good, the holy, by "an effort of the will, the fruit of the human spirit permeated by the Spirit of God."[106] In this struggle between good and evil, between the desires of the flesh, on the one hand, and the requirements of purity, self-mastery, and true freedom, on the other, "man proves himself stronger, thanks to the power of the Holy Spirit."[107] In a word, he attains holiness and freedom through purity and self-mastery, which are attained through the work of the Spirit, that is, by God's grace.

3. What Is Freedom?

The understanding of freedom portrayed in St. Paul's works and implicit in Christ's teaching is not the common understanding of freedom prevalent today. Most people would regard freedom as the right to do what one pleases. For most people, freedom means an absence of any constraint and, more fundamentally, the right to do as one pleases at any particular time. St. Paul would disagree with this view of freedom. He would agree that freedom involves the opportunity to choose without external constraint; but, he would point out, if one uses one's opportunities to choose sin, one falls under internal constraints, and so loses one's inner freedom. St. Paul addresses this issue when he writes, "For you were called for freedom, brothers. But do not use this freedom as an opportunity for the flesh; rather, serve one another through love."[108] By giving in to the flesh, that is, by living according to the flesh, we allow our freedom to be taken over by our passions and emotions. Then we are no longer free, in the sense that we direct our passions and emotions; rather, they direct us. They constitute, in effect, an interior compulsion that deprives us of true inner freedom. If we cannot say no, our yes doesn't mean anything.

In Mozart's famous opera *Don Giovanni*, Don Giovanni declares his freedom to do what he pleases. However, this freedom translates into murder, fornication, adultery, and lying and eventually results in spiritual death. The unrepentant libertine descends at the end of the opera into the fiery pit of hell. The great composer, with the librettist, Lorenzo da Ponte, contrasts Don Giovanni's claim of freedom with the actual situation: Don Giovanni is chained by his passions and, in effect, after a long life of following those passions, is subject to them even when, one suspects, he would rather not follow them. He doesn't have the strength to ignore his passions, and so he is not free; therefore, his yes is meaningless.

Don Giovanni experienced spiritual death. Quoting St. Paul from his Letter to the Galatians, John Paul reminds us in address 52 that life according to the flesh leads to death, and life according to the Spirit leads to life. The pope connects the death that St. Paul spoke about with grave sin, which the church has called "mortal." He also repeats the point that freedom is the result of the effort of self-mastery and purity.

The "effort of the will permeated by the Spirit" results in self-mastery. In other words, the will, through purity, orchestrates the senses to respond to the gospel value system. The will masters the desires of the world and the flesh by turning these desires toward the values presented by the gospel. Thus a desire for union, sexual or otherwise, is turned by the will into love—love of spouse, children, God. Freedom exists for love. Without freedom, there could be no love. But such a noble calling requires self-mastery, which results in true freedom.

Obviously, however, people can understand freedom to mean the power to do anything at all, even to embrace the desires of the flesh, as Don Giovanni did. But Don Giovanni offers an example of someone who exercised his free will as a power to do whatever he wanted, but was enslaved by his choices.

If free will can be used to enslave ourselves and reject God, why did God give us free will in the first place? The answer is clear: without free will, there cannot be love. God gave us freedom so that we could love. Wishing us to be able to love him and others, he risked sin, that is, he allowed for the possibility that we would misuse our freedom and reject him. Love was so important that God gave us freedom, even though we could reject him through that very freedom. From the cross of Christ, we can understand most profoundly how terrible sin is. Likewise, from the cross we can glimpse faintly how important it is to God that we have the power to love him and others. Since free will is necessary for us to love, God gave us free will even at the risk of the cross, by which he would ultimately redeem us from our misuse of freedom. Thus God risked everything for love.

With this emphasis on love from St. Paul, we come back to Christ—to his Sermon on the Mount and, even more, to his passion and death. What greater example of love, achieved through self-mastery, could there be? The famous prayer in Gethsemane at the outset of the passion tells it all: "Not my will but yours be done."[109] Love is a union of wills. Christ joined his human will with the divine will, with his Father's will. This union was achieved by means of a victory of his human will over the bodily fear and horror that he felt. This self-mastery was the most stupendous act of love the world has ever seen. There can be no greater example of purity of heart and holiness. Let us always, each and every one of us, try to imitate his splendid example.

N. PURITY AND THE BODY: ADDRESSES 54 TO 57

With the help of the Holy Spirit, men and women, although afflicted by the effects of original sin, can achieve a self-mastery that gives them the freedom to love as they should, that is, with a complete donation of themselves.

In address 54 John Paul quotes 1 Thessalonians: "This is the will of God, your sanctification: that you abstain from unchastity, that each one of you know how to control his own body in holiness and honor, not in the passion of lust like heathens who do not know God (1 Th 4:3-5)."[110] John Paul remarks that in this passage, the apostle to the gentiles is speaking about purity. The pope then defines purity as a capacity; that is, a virtue. A virtue is a power to act in a certain way. For example, the virtue of faith gives one the power to affirm revealed truths, such as the existence of the Trinity. Purity gives men and women the capability of living chastely. In other words, purity is the supernatural virtue that allows us to achieve the self-mastery so essential to freedom, which, in turn, is essential for love. This point, of course, is very much within the Catholic theological tradition, especially in the thought of St. Thomas Aquinas.

1. Purity and Control

The pope goes on to say in address 54 that through purity we are enabled to control our own body—and the bodies of others, especially those of the opposite sex—in holiness and honor. Obviously, if purity results in self-mastery, with the help of God's grace, then purity helps us control ourselves. The pope writes, "Consequently it can be admitted that control of one's body (and indirectly that of others) in holiness and honor confers adequate meaning and value on that abstention."[111] Here, of course, the pope reasons that purity leads to self-mastery—what in this passage he calls "control." The reason for abstaining is so that we can honor ourselves and others by recognizing the incredible dignity and value that we all have not just in our interior being but, most especially, in the human body as the expression of the person.

In address 55 John Paul connects purity to the remarks of St. Paul about how we endow the less-presentable parts of our bodies with greater modesty and honor.[112] These parts of the body need greater honor and modesty not because in themselves they are any different than any other parts of the body but because we feel a certain shame in their regard. This shame is an "echo," as the pope writes, of the shame of Adam and Eve after sin. As heirs of our first parents who suffer the effects of original sin, we too feel their shame. "As a result of discord in the body, some parts are considered weaker, less honorable, and so unpresentable. This discord is a further expression of the vision of man's interior state after original sin; that is, of historical man. The man of original innocence, male and female, did not feel that discord in the body,"[113] because there was no discord. We can overcome the discord of the body caused by original sin, that is, we can be transformed, through purity of heart.

Underlining his point in address 56, the pope writes that "purity is a capacity centered on the dignity of the body. That is, it is centered on the dignity of the person in relation to his own body, to the femininity or masculinity which is manifested in this body."[114] Since purity allows us to recognize and relate to our masculinity or femininity in holiness and honor, it is, as the pope wrote in the previous address, indirectly a means of holding the bodies of others in holiness and honor. Regarding ourselves in holiness and honor, we will hold the bodies of others, especially those of the opposite sex, in holiness and honor also.

2. Human Dignity and Value

The burden of address 56 is to show that while each of us has an infinite honor and dignity from God's creation of each of us in his own image and likeness, we are infinitely more valuable because we share the same human nature as God himself possessed in Christ. "Human nature, by the very fact that it was assumed, not absorbed, in Him, has been raised in us also to a dignity beyond compare. For, by his Incarnation, he, the Son of God, in a certain way united Himself with each man."[115] Since God shared our humanity and did everything we do except sin, then everything we do except sin, and indeed everything we are, is worthy of God himself. We are incredibly valuable by our creation in God's image, but this infinite worth and dignity has been increased immeasurably and unbelievably, because God united himself with each of us through the incarnation. Thus, "Christ has imprinted on the human body—on the body of every man and every woman—new dignity."[116] In addition, each of us, while we are in the state grace, has the Holy Spirit within us. All this means that we belong to Christ, as St. Paul says, and that, if we defile our bodies, we defile Christ and act against the dignity of the Holy Spirit!

In address 57 John Paul teaches that while the Holy Spirit gives us the virtues, including purity, through grace, the Holy Spirit also confers on us his seven gifts, including the gift of piety. The supernatural virtues, given with sanctifying grace, enable our faculties—our mind, will, and body—to focus on the divine. For example, the supernatural virtue of faith allows the mind to accept the supernatural truths of the faith. The virtues of temperance and purity allow us to control our bodies in accord not only with the demands of living well on earth but also with the demands of life lived according to the ultimate goal, heaven. There are natural virtues of temperance and purity, which were discussed by the pagan Greek philosophers. There are also supernatural virtues of temperance and purity. The difference between the two types of virtue is in their purposes. The natural virtues help us regulate our lives here on earth with others. The supernatural virtues, while including everything the natural powers do, also help us regulate our lives in light of our ultimate goal, heaven. For example, the virgin or celibate regulates his or her relations with others through the natural virtue of purity, but also, clearly, makes use of the supernatural virtue of purity to express the love of God.

The gifts of the Holy Spirit operate seamlessly with the supernatural virtues. The gifts affect not so much the objects of our acts as how our human faculties operate. As a person grows in the exercise of the divine life, his or her faculties, sharing the gifts of the Holy Spirit, are more and more enabled to operate not just in a human way but in a divine way. So we come to believe truths not in a discursive, reasoning way but to believe them in the way that God knows them. That is, our intellects, perfected by the gifts, operate more and more the way God's intellect operates. Even with the gifts, we never attain to knowing precisely as God knows or loving precisely as God loves. But the gifts allow our operations to become more and more like the divine operations.

Purity is a virtue, a capacity, that allows us to control our own bodies for the sake of the kingdom of heaven. Piety, one of the seven gifts of the

Holy Spirit, allows us to exercise the virtue of purity—to do this work, this operation—through our minds and wills in the way God would do it, that is, the way Christ did. Piety "makes the human subject sensitive to that dignity which is characteristic of the human body by virtue of the mystery of creation and redemption."[117] John Paul means here that through the gift of piety the human body is truly able to express a Godlike love in a Godlike way, that is, to love as God loves.

The pope ends address 57 with a brief reference to the Old Testament. He demonstrates that the gift of wisdom is a condition for purity, in the sense that unless one recognizes the reason for purity, that is, the profound dignity of the human person conferred through creation *and* redemption, there is no reason to attempt to be pure. The recognition of our value and dignity given to us by creation and redemption comes through wisdom.

The conclusion of these addresses on purity is found about the middle of address 57: "Purity is the glory of the human body before God. It is God's glory in the human body, through which masculinity and femininity are manifested. From purity springs that extraordinary beauty which permeates every sphere of men's common life and makes it possible to express in it simplicity and depth, cordiality and the unrepeatable authenticity of personal trust."[118]

O. SUMMARY OF THE SECOND CYCLE: ADDRESSES 58 TO 59

These two audiences are a sweeping summary of everything the pope has said in the first two cycles of the theology of the body. It is probably best simply to follow John Paul's points in the order he makes them.[119]

- Christ taught that no one should commit adultery (address 58, first paragraph, p. 210).
- Christ also taught that no one should divorce his wife, because it was not that way "in the beginning" (address 58, first paragraph, p. 211).
- This teaching of Christ led John Paul to the first two chapters of Genesis and his penetrating analysis of what the beginning was like (address 58, second paragraph, p. 211).

- But we are not in that situation now, so the truths from the analysis of the beginning need to be applied to us as "historical" men and women, in accordance with our situation (address 58, third paragraph, pp. 211–12).
- We also need to understand the context for those who heard Christ give his teaching on adultery; that is, his analysis of the Old Testament traditions (address 58, third paragraph, pp. 211–12).
- Christ's words are true and normative, that is, they are guides for behavior. But to fulfill this norm requires purity of heart (address 58, fourth paragraph, p. 212).
- Regarding Christ's words on adultery in the heart, "It can be affirmed that, with their expressive evangelical eloquence, the man of original innocence is, in a way, recalled to the consciousness of the man of lust" (address 58, fifth paragraph, p. 212). In other words, the norms in paradise for Adam and Eve are applied by Christ to those of us who have inherited original sin. The norms of paradise are possible because of purity!
- But we must open ourselves to this purity. It requires an interior action by each of us (address 58, sixth paragraph, pp. 212–13).
- Purity allows us to discover the dignity of the body, so that we do not treat it as a thing through lust (address 58, seventh paragraph, p. 213).
- Piety gives an ease and joy at the victory over lust and allows the appreciation of the great gift of the human body to human persons (address 58, eighth paragraph, pp. 213–14).
- Christ speaks to every single human being (address 59, first paragraph, p. 214).
- The theology of the body, developed from Christ's words, is a pedagogy—an education in how to act (address 59, second paragraph, p. 214).
- "The Creator has assigned as a task to man his body, his masculinity and femininity" (address 59, second paragraph, p. 214).
- The human body is the manifestation of the human person. Therefore the body cannot be grasped simply in terms of its biological functions (address 59, third paragraph, p. 215).
- The modern sciences of biology and medicine sometimes divorce what is spiritual from what is biological and thus do not have an integral view of the human person (address 59, fourth paragraph, p. 215).

- This situation is corrected by the theology of the body (address 59, fifth paragraph, p. 215).
- Modern science can help us discover the true meaning of the body "only if it is accompanied by an adequate spiritual maturity of the human person" (address 59, sixth paragraph, pp. 215–16).
- The modern pronouncements of the church: Pope Paul VI's encyclical *Humanae Vitae* (On Human Life) and *Gaudium et Spes* (Pastoral Constitution on the Church in the Modern World) confirm this point of view (address 59, seventh and eighth paragraphs, p. 216).
- These quotations reflect the very words of Christ (address 59, ninth paragraph, p. 216).
- We can fulfill these demands, as Pope Paul VI teaches in his encyclical (address 59, tenth paragraph, p. 217).
- But the theology of the body is required, because it is a pedagogy of the body (address 59, eleventh paragraph, p. 217).
- One last note: before we conclude this cycle, we need to consider the human body in art in our present, historical situation (address 59, twelfth paragraph, p. 217).

P. THE HUMAN BODY IN ART: ADDRESSES 60 TO 63

The last four addresses of the second cycle are by way of an addendum. This addendum discusses a very important issue: the portrayal of the human body in arts such as sculpture and painting; in the performing arts of theater, ballet, and concerts; and in the mass media of television and film. If the body is the expression of an individual person, then portraying it as an anonymous figure—as in sculpture or photography—becomes somewhat of a problem. It is this difficulty that the pope addresses in these last addresses of the second cycle.

Art ennobles and enriches our lives. A musician once said that art was the grandchild of God: God creates human persons, and human persons fashion art.[120] Art is the grandchild of God in another way as well: God created the world, while art takes from the world materials for its craft—stones for architecture, sounds for music, colors for painting, and so on. Art also takes from the world subjects for itself. The painter portrays landscapes or animal scenes. The architect takes pleasant shapes found in creation and combines them to create buildings. God created the world; the artist fashions his work from the created world.

1. The Human Person as a Subject of Art

The most interesting subject for art is the human person, because the human person is the most fascinating and intriguing being created by God on earth. Some of the most respected masterworks of human art are representations of the human person: Michelangelo's *David*, Leonardo da Vinci's *Mona Lisa*, Mozart's operas *Le Nozze di Figaro* and *Don Giovanni*, Shakespeare's tragedies, and so on. Further, since art is perceived through the five senses, the artistic masterworks concerned with the human person always represent the visible, audible, material aspect of the human person, the human body.

The body is the expression of the individual person and belongs to the individual. Each of us experiences his or her being, including his or her body, in a subjective way. That is, we know ourselves (we watch ourselves through our self-awareness, our consciousness) as embodied beings. But when, for example, the human body is painted or sculpted, it is divorced from the individual person and becomes an object, a thing we see. "Therefore, . . . in the given case, it is a question of the objectivized body."[121] In other words, through art, the human body becomes not the expression of an individual person but rather something divorced from the person that is viewed as a thing. This happens in one way in the plastic arts, such as sculpture and painting; in a different way in the performing arts, such as plays, ballet, and concerts; and in a third way through television and film.

2. Art and the Nuptial Meaning of the Body

In addition to divorcing the body from the person, art can violate the significance of the body as a sign and means of a personal donation of one person to another. In address 61 the pope reminds us that the human body "has the meaning of a gift of the person to the person."[122] Here, of course, John Paul is referring to his thesis that through our self-awareness we experience our bodies as created to be a gift to another person: men realize through their self-awareness that their masculinity is designed to be a gift to the feminine, and women realize that their femininity is designed to be a gift to the masculine. This is what John Paul has called the nuptial meaning of the body. But "the artistic objectivization of the human body in its male and female nakedness, in order to make it first of all a model and then the subject of the work of art, is always to a certain extent a going outside of this original and, for the body, its specific configuration of interpersonal donation. In a way, that constitutes an uprooting of the human body from this configuration."[123] Through art, not only is the body divorced from the individual person, but its meaning of interpersonal donation can also be distorted and even falsified. It ceases to be the means of a gift of one person to another and becomes an anonymous "gift" to everyone. As the pope is quick to add, "The fact that this problem is raised does not mean that the human body, in its nakedness, cannot become a subject of works of art, but only that this problem is not purely aesthetic, nor morally indifferent."[124] He means that the portrayal of the human body in art must be subject to norms outside of the discipline of the particular art involved. Such portrayals must take into account the entire personal system of values that the pope has taught us in the theology of the body.

3. The Role of Shame in Artistic Portrayals of the Human Person

In address 61 the pope reminds us of the nature of shame. As he has previously taught,[125] shame exists when we act contrary to an important value that we hold. Since shame is unpleasant, people try to avoid it. Therefore, shame encourages us to act in accordance with our value system. Shame then has a double function: it testifies to the continued existence in a human person's mind of a particular value, and it encourages the person to act in accordance with that value. Adam and Eve experienced shame when they discovered they were naked after their sin.

Shame at nakedness is still very much a part of the human condition, and it continues to protect the basic dignity of the human person, who through his or her body, is to become a gift to another. We experience a certain uneasiness, a shame, when we need to undress for a physical exam or medical test. John Paul points out how the deprivation of clothing can be used to strip away human dignity, as in concentration camps.

When a work of art violates what the pope calls "the limit of shame," the work of art is no longer in accordance with human dignity. When does art cease to be art and become what the pope calls pornovision or pornography? He answers his own question. These things take place "when those deep governing rules of the gift and of mutual donation, which are inscribed in this femininity and masculinity through the whole structure of the human being, are violated."[126]

4. The Importance of the Intention of the Artist and the Recipient

The title of address 62—"Art Must Not Violate the Right to Privacy"—sums up John Paul II's thesis in these last four addresses of the second cycle. How does the violation occur? "The deep inscription of the meaning of the human body," that is, its creation for a self-gift to another, "can be violated only in the intentional order of the reproduction and the representation."[127] The violation occurs in the intention of the artist and in the intention of the one looking. If the artist—painter, sculptor, film director—wants to violate the meaning of the body, then that violation usually occurs. If those viewing the artistic reproduction of the body intend to see it that way, then the meaning of the body can also be violated. If an artist has an improper intention (or even if the artist lacks talent or skill and therefore, even with the best intention, cannot achieve what he or she wishes) then "that 'element of the gift' is, so to speak, suspended in the dimension of an unknown reception and an unforeseen response."[128] The whole problem of depicting the human body, especially the naked human body, in art "is not the effect of a puritanical mentality or of a narrow moralism, just as it is not the product of a thought imbued with Manichaeism. It is a question of an extremely important, fundamental sphere of values"[129]—that is, the dignity of the human person in his or her body/person unity.

But the human body is portrayed as naked in art, even in the literature of the Scriptures, as, for example, Adam and Eve in Genesis and the bride and the groom in the Song of Songs. So it must be possible to portray in art what John Paul calls the "full truth of man" in his body/person unity. Of course, it is. It demands an artist with talent and training *and* with the intention to tell the full truth about man. "In the course of the various eras, beginning from antiquity—and above all in the great period of Greek classical art—there are works of art whose subject is the human body in its nakedness. The contemplation of this makes it possible to concentrate, in a way, on the whole truth of man, on the dignity and the beauty—also the 'suprasensual' beauty—of his masculinity and femininity. These works bear within them, almost hidden, an element of sublimation. This leads the viewer, through the body, to the whole personal mystery of man. In contact with these works, where we do not feel drawn by their content to 'looking lustfully,' . . . we learn in a way that nuptial meaning of the body which corresponds to, and is the measure of, 'purity of heart.'"[130] Certainly, works such as the *Venus de Milo* and *Winged Victory* from antiquity would be included among the works that capture the suprasensual beauty of the human person; so would Michelangelo's magnificent *David*—to mention only three of many such works.

But it is not just the artist who needs talent, training, and the proper intention; it is also the viewer. Even the most beautiful works of art, capturing the truth of the human person, can be viewed in a way that is not responsible; that is, that does not attempt to see the full truth of the human person. In a certain way, the great artists who attempt to capture the truth of the human person have assigned a task, that is, the task of seeing this full truth in their works, "to the viewer and, in the wider range, to every recipient of the work."[131]

In these remarks on art, John Paul is developing and echoing a plea made by Pope Paul VI in his famous "birth control" encyclical, *Humanae Vitae* (On Human Life). In address 63 John Paul quotes Pope Paul VI's plea to artists and those who appreciate art "to create an atmosphere favorable to education in chastity."[132] Art, especially photography and films, and the media of art, television and the Internet, have a serious obligation to portray the human body as having the meaning of a self-donation. It is only from such a realization that chastity—the ability in each of us to make a self-donation to another—develops. In our age of ever-increasing temptations to look at the human body as an object, especially through inappropriate images available on the Internet, the words of Pope Paul VI, and even more those of Pope John Paul II in these last four addresses of the second cycle of the theology of the body, could not be more important.

Q. Conclusion of the Second Cycle

With these last reflections on the depiction of the human body in works of art, John Paul concludes his extensive second cycle of the theology of the body. In the first cycle (addresses 1–23), he analyzed the words of Christ in response to the Pharisees' question about divorce. In the second cycle (addresses 24 –63), he took up Christ's words in the Sermon on the Mount about adultery, lustful looks, and adultery in the heart. The third cycle (addresses 64–72) takes up the words of Christ in response to the Sadducees who come to him and put the question about a woman who married seven brothers in turn. The Sadducees ask, "At the resurrection whose wife shall she be?"[133] The first words of Christ about divorce, with his reference to "the beginning," led the pope to an analysis of Adam and Eve before sin. Christ's teaching regarding adultery led the pope to consider the state of historical man, the state of all of us subject to original sin and its effects. The words of Christ about marriage and the resurrection allow John Paul to discuss the way we will be in heaven after the resurrection of the body. The first cycle considered the human person in his and her body/person structure, before sin. The second cycle considered the human body/person structure after sin. The third cycle will consider the human body/person structure in the resurrection, when we will reign gloriously with God in heaven at the end of the world. There are then three ways that the human body expresses the person: in the state of innocence before sin (the distant past), in the state of sin on earth (the present), and in the resurrection (the future). The next chapter will take up the third cycle of the theology of the body.

1. See Matthew 5:27-28. John Paul adds, "According to ancient translations, the text is: . . . 'has already made her an adultress in his heart,' a formula which seems to be more exact."

2. See TB, no. 24, p. 103 (1).

3. See TB, no. 25, p. 106 (2).

4. See TB, no. 25, p. 108 (5).

5. See TB, no. 24, p. 105 (4).

6. See TB, no. 24, p. 105 (4).

7. See TB, no. 24, p. 105 (4).

8. See TB, no. 24, p. 104 (2). See also no. 42, p. 153 (2), where John Paul states that Jesus enunciates the commandment "in order to show how it must be understood and put into practice, so that the justice that God-Yahweh wished as legislator may abound in it. It is in order that it may abound to a greater extent than appeared from the interpretation and casuistry of the Old Testament doctors."

9. See TB, no. 24, p. 105 (3).

10. See Matthew 5:28.

11. See 1 John 2:16-17.

12. See TB, no. 26, p. 109 (2).

13. See TB, no. 26, p. 109 (2).

14. See TB, no. 26, p. 109 (2).

15. See Genesis 3:4-5.

16. See Matthew 4:9.

17. See TB, no. 26, pp. 110–11 (4).

18. See Genesis 2:25.

19. See Genesis 3:7.

20. See TB, no. 27, p. 112 (1).

21. See TB, no. 27, p. 112 (2).

22. See TB, no. 27, p. 113 (4).

23. See Genesis 2:16-17.

24. See the discussion of address 28 below.

25. See TB, no. 27, p. 114 (4).

26. See TB, no. 28, p. 115 (2).

27. See TB, no. 28, pp. 115–16 (4).

28. See Romans 7:23.

29. See TB, no. 29, p. 117 (2).

30. See TB, no. 29, p. 118 (2).

31. See TB, no. 29, p. 118 (2).

32. See TB, no. 29, p. 119 (3).

33. See TB, no. 29, p. 119 (5).

34. See TB, no. 28, p. 117 (6).

35. See TB, no. 28, p. 117 (6).

36. See TB, no. 30, p. 120 (3).

37. See TB, no. 30, p. 121 (5).

38. See TB, no. 31, p. 123 (3).

39. See TB, no. 31, p. 123 (3).

40. See TB, no. 31, p. 123 (3).

41. See TB, no. 32, p. 126 (2).

42. See TB, no. 32, p. 126 (3).

43. See TB, no. 32, p. 126 (3).

44. See TB, no. 32, p. 127 (6).

45. See TB, no. 32, p. 127 (5).

46. See Genesis 2:23-25.

47. See TB, no. 33, pp. 128–29 (2).

48. See Matthew 5:27-28.

49. See above, p. 71.

50. See TB, no. 34, p. 131 (2).

51. See TB, no. 34, p. 132 (2).

52. See TB, no. 34, p. 132 (4).

53. See TB, no. 34, p. 132 (4).

54. Polygamy and other such violations of the original intent of the Creator as are contained in the Old Testament were permitted by God as exceptions only because the Old Testament people were not ready to accept the full weight of the truth of the moral code.

55. See TB, no. 35, p. 133 (1).

56. See TB, no. 36, p. 136 (2).

57. See TB, no. 36, p. 137 (3).

58. See TB, no. 36, p. 137 (5).

59. See TB, no. 37, p. 141 (5).

60. See TB, no 38, p. 144 (6).

61. See TB, no. 38, p. 144 (5).

62. See TB, no. 38, p. 144 (5).

63. See TB, no. 39, p. 147 (4).

64. See TB, no. 40, p. 149 (3).

65. See TB, no. 40, p. 149 (4).

66. See TB, no. 40, p. 150 (5).

67. See TB, no. 41, pp. 151–52 (4).

68. See Wojtyla, *Love and Responsibility*, p. 41.

69. See TB, no. 42, p. 156 (7).

70. See TB, no. 43, p. 157 (3). When the pope said this at the general audience of October 8, 1980, there was considerable response from around the world. The idea that a husband could commit adultery with his own wife shocked many people and disturbed some lawyers and state leaders, because laws defined adultery as an act of sexual intercourse between a married man or woman with someone who was not his or her spouse.

71. See TB, no. 44, p. 160 (1).

72. See TB, no. 44, p. 160 (3).

73. See TB, no. 44, p. 162 (6).

74. See TB, no. 45, p. 163 (1).

75. See TB, no. 45, p. 163 (3).

76. See TB, no. 45, pp. 163–64 (3).

77. See TB, no. 44, p. 162 (6).

78. See Genesis 1:31.

79. See TB, no. 45, p. 165 (5).

80. See TB, no. 46, p. 167 (4).

81. See TB, no. 46, p. 168 (6).

82. See TB, no. 47, p. 169 (2).

83. See TB, no, 47, p. 170 (4).

84. See TB, no. 47, p. 171 (5).

85. See TB, no. 48, p. 171 (1).

86. See TB, no. 48, p. 173 (4).

87. See TB, no. 48, p. 173 (5).

88. See TB, no. 48, p. 173 (5).

89. See TB, no. 48, p. 173 (4).

90. See TB, no. 49, p. 176 (5).

91. See TB, no. 49, p. 177 (7).

92. See TB, no. 50, p. 178 (3).

93. See TB, no. 50, p. 179 (4).

94. See TB, no. 51, p. 191 (1).

95. See TB, no. 51, p. 193 (5).

96. See Matthew 15:18-19.

97. See Galatians 5:17.

98. See TB, no. 52, p. 195 (2).

99. See Galatians 5:19-21.

100. See Galatians 5:22-23.

101. See Matthew 15:18.

102. See Romans 8:13.

103. See TB, no. 51, p. 191 (1).

104. See TB, no. 28, p. 115 (2).

105. See Romans 7:19.

106. See TB, no 51, p. 193 (5).

107. See TB, no. 51, p. 194 (5).

108. See Galatians 5:13.

109. See Luke 22:42, New Revised Standard Version.

110. See TB, no. 54, p. 200 (1).

111. See TB, no. 54, p. 201 (3).

112. See 1 Corinthians 12:18, 22-25.

113. See TB, no. 55, p. 204 (6).

114. See TB, no. 56, pp. 205–6 (1).

115. See *Redemptor Hominis*, 8.

116. See TB, no. 56, p. 207 (4).

117. See TB, no. 57, p. 208 (2).

118. See TB, no. 57, p. 209 (3).

119. See TB, nos. 58–59, pp. 210–17.

120. Monsignor Richard J. Schuler, St. Paul, MN, *viva voce* to the author.

121. See TB, no. 60, p. 218 (2).

122. See TB, no. 61, p. 220 (1).

123. See TB, no. 61, p. 221 (1).

124. See TB, no. 61, p. 221 (1).

125. See TB, no. 29.

126. See TB, no. 61, p. 223 (4).

127. See TB, no. 62, p. 224 (2).

128. See TB, no. 62, p. 225 (3).

129. See TB, no. 62, p. 225 (4).

130. See TB, no. 63, pp. 227–28 (5).

131. See TB, no. 63, p. 229 (7).

132. See TB, no. 63, p. 228 (6).

133. See Mark 12:23.

The Resurrection
of the Body

General Audience Addresses 64 to 72

A. Introduction

On May 13, 1981, a week after the pope concluded the second cycle of the theology of the body series (addresses 24 to 63) and presumably the day he planned to begin the third cycle on the resurrection of the body (64 to 72), he was shot in St. Peter's Square by Mehmet Ali Agca. The bullet hit the pope before the audience had formally begun, as he was touring the square and greeting the crowd assembled for the Wednesday audience, in his specially built jeep, the so-called "popemobile." At these Wednesday audiences, the pope would normally make one or two circuits of the square in the popemobile. In this way, he could interact with the crowd and they could greet him, before he took his seat on the raised platform in front of the basilica to begin the audience. On May 13, just after the pope had returned a little girl to her parents, and as the popemobile headed toward the platform, shots rang out.

The pope suddenly slumped into the arms of his longtime secretary, Monsignor (now Cardinal) Stanislaw Dziwisz. John Paul was rushed to Gemelli hospital. Miraculously, the bullets from Agca's gun missed major arteries and nerve centers, but John Paul was for a time close to death from the loss of blood. Through the skill of surgeons, he gradually recovered, only to be felled in June by a viral infection. By early fall, he had regained much of his strength, but the third cycle of the theology of the body series did not begin until the Wednesday audience of November 11, 1981.

The assassination attempt on John Paul II gives his great principle that the body is the expression of the person a concrete reality. The pope's body was attacked, but it was his person that was wounded. The person, not just his body, was near death. When the body is touched, it is the person who is touched, because the body and person form one entity, one human being. Near death, suffering the real possibility of the separation of his body and his spirit, or soul, the pope experienced in a very direct way what death means for the human person. Death is the separation of soul and body. But the resurrection will be the reunion of soul and body. In facing death, the pope also faced the certainty of the resurrection. His teaching on the resurrection of the body, certainly already formulated and written by this time, took on an experiential reality for him.

B. THE SADDUCEES' QUESTION: ADDRESSES 64 TO 65

The pope begins the third cycle without reference to the assassination attempt or his wounds. He simply says, "After a rather long pause, today we will resume the meditations . . . on the theology of the body."[1] Having already considered two previous "words" of Christ—the one regarding divorce, which was occasioned by the Pharisees' question about the Old Testament practice of allowing a man to divorce his wife, and the one about "looking lustfully," from the Sermon on the Mount—the pope now takes up a third "word" of Christ relating to the body: the one in response to the Sadducees' question about the resurrection of the body. The Pharisees' question on divorce led John Paul to the study of the body/person unity before sin. The "word" from the Sermon on the Mount led him to analyze the body/person unity after sin and before the resurrection. The "word" to the Sadducees leads the pope here to an analysis of the body/person unity in heaven after the resurrection of the body.

Some Sadducees came up to Christ one day and tried to trap him. They did not believe in the resurrection of the body, and they knew that he did. Through their question, they hoped to make it appear that the resurrection of the body was impossible.

In the Old Testament, there was a law that if a man died without children, his brother should marry the widow and preserve his brother's line by giving his widow children.[2] Based on this law, the Sadducees present a hypothetical case. There was a woman and seven brothers. She married the oldest brother, who died without children. She then married the second brother, who also died without children. In the end, she married all seven brothers, all of whom died childless. Finally, the woman died. The Sadducees asked Christ, "In the resurrection, therefore, to which of the seven will she be wife? For they all had her."[3]

Of course, the Sadducees' case turns on the question of the human body. Marriage is very much a bodily reality: a union of two persons expressed through the flesh. Husbands and wives, after all, become one flesh. The resurrection is also a bodily reality: the reunion of soul and body. If there is a resurrection of the body, that is, if there are bodies in heaven, then, the Sadducees suggested, there must be a possibility of marriage after the resurrection. But if a wife were married more than once on earth, that is, if she were one flesh with more than one husband, to whom would she be joined in one flesh in heaven? The Sadducees were arguing that the earthly, bodily reality of marriage would necessarily be extended to heaven if there was a bodily resurrection. Implicitly the Sadducees claimed that the body/soul unity on earth would be identical to the body/soul unity in heaven. Since it is impossible for the woman with seven husbands to be married to more than one husband simultaneously on earth, so also in heaven. Since she married seven times, she would be married in heaven to seven husbands simultaneously. But this is impossible. Therefore, there can be no marriage in heaven. If there is no marriage in heaven, there is no body/soul unity in heaven; that is, there is no resurrection of the body.

After presenting the Sadducees' case in address 64, John Paul in 65 analyzes the Sadducees' intentions in presenting this case to Christ and Christ's intentions in his answer, "When they rise from the dead, they neither marry nor are given in marriage."[4] Of course, in his answer, Christ denied the basic premise. He teaches that the body/soul unity of a particular person in heaven is not identical to the body/soul unity of that same person on earth.

C. A New System of Forces in the Human Person: Addresses 66 to 69

In address 66, the pope speaks about the effects of the resurrection on the human body: "The resurrection means . . . a completely new state of human life itself."[5] It means a "spiritualization of his somatic nature." The resurrection means the establishment "of another 'system of forces' within man. The resurrection means a new submission of the body to the spirit."[6] Christ says that those who attain to the resurrection of the dead "cannot die any more because they are equal to angels."[7] This correlates with the statement from the psalms that even now, on earth, in the historical state of man after sin, we are "little less than the angels" (Psalm 8:5).[8]

1. The Spiritualization of the Body in Heaven

In address 67 John Paul elaborates on what he means by spiritualization. "Spiritualization means not only that the spirit will dominate the body, but, I would say, that it will fully permeate the body, and that the forces of the spirit will permeate the energies of the body."[9] This new spiritualization of the body will have its source in a "divinization" of each person's humanity. The divine life of grace, given in baptism, will be perfectly united with human life, to the extent that grace will permeate every aspect of humanity. "Participation in divine nature, participation in the interior life of God Himself, penetration and permeation of what is essentially human by what is essentially divine, will then reach its peak, so that the life of the human spirit will arrive at such fullness which previously had been absolutely inaccessible to it."[10] The spiritualization of every aspect of the human person has as its source grace, which will make us, in every aspect of our persons, sharers in the life of God. This divinization of all powers and capacities of human nature includes the body. "When Christ speaks of the resurrection, he proves at the same time that the human body will also take part, in its way, in this eschatological experience of truth and love, united with the vision of God face to face."[11]

2. A Total Concentration on God

The pope's description of the joy of the human person in his or her body/soul unity in heaven is difficult to grasp, because no one living on earth has ever experienced it or anything close to it. Further, not everything about this state has been revealed to us. Nevertheless, it is clear that we will be so taken up by the vision of God, so permeated by the divine itself, that every capacity and power we have will be completely and forever focused on him. Nothing else will interest us or attract us. For brief moments on earth and in a much less intense way, most of us have experienced something like what the pope is describing. We lose ourselves in the beauty of nature; we are awed by the power of a storm, volcano, or earthquake; we are so intent on a loved one that nothing will intrude on our concentration. These are very pale, imperfect reflections of what the pope is trying to describe.

In more theological terms, we can understand Christ's words about the resurrection of the body as the complete fulfillment of the nuptial meaning of the body. The human body reveals to human persons through its nuptial meaning that we are called to love, to give ourselves in imitation of the Trinity. The nuptial meaning of the body is the understanding in each of our intellects that we are created to give ourselves to one another in a Godlike self-giving, life-affirming, and life-giving love. Husbands and wives give concrete reality to the nuptial meaning of the body by living a loving union expressed in and through their bodily self-giving. The marital embrace is not only an expression of the spouses' love; it also enriches their union and allows their mutual affection to grow and intensify.

In heaven, the nuptial meaning of the body, that is, the understanding that we are to love, will be expressed and lived not through bodily union with a spouse but through the "penetration and permeation of what is essentially human by what is essentially divine."[12] Once established, the union between each person and God will not need to grow or intensify, because it reaches its pinnacle at the very first moment of the union and remains at that point. Therefore, one of the aspects of the marital embrace, the intensification of the loving union of the spouses, will not be needed.

As John Paul teaches in address 68, the human body will participate in this union with God because every bodily power will be completely fixed on God. The joy of the divinization will translate itself into a bodily expression that, in turn, will completely absorb every bodily human power. Describing the human person who experiences the resurrection in heaven, John Paul writes, "There will be born in him a love of such depth and power of concentration on God himself, as to completely absorb his whole psychosomatic subjectivity."[13]

As a very imperfect image of the bodily absorption in the union with God, one might think of a child who hears some glorious news, for example, the family is going on vacation to Disney World, and can do nothing but dance in a wild whirling motion for a few minutes. The child is completely focused on the joy of the news and is oblivious to the family members around him or her. The same absorption often occurs in young children on Christmas. They become so completely focused on the gifts as to be almost oblivious to every request their parents might make. Similarly, the sheer, constant joy of the union with God will so absorb us that every sense and power of our bodies will be focused on God. The absorption in God will be so intense that we will be oblivious to everything else. This absorption of the bodily powers in the union with God is foreshadowed in a dim way by the mystical experiences of saints who have been so taken up in prayer, that is, in union with God, that they have been oblivious to time, to noises around them, even to physical pain.

We might also understand the absorption of the bodily powers in the union with God in light of the surge in our emotions that the vision of God face to face will cause. The union with God in heaven is one of love. Love certainly involves the emotional powers of the body. It is obvious to most people after a deeply emotional experience that the physical powers of the human body are intimately tied to one's emotions. We often speak of "not bringing outside problems onto the field," because an emotional focus on such problems can distract us from the activity at hand and actually interfere with our physical performance. We also talk of "not bringing the office home," because, again, our concern with work-related issues can divert our attention from our family members and affect how we relate—or don't relate—to them. These sayings reflect our awareness that emotions play a huge part in the exercise of our physical powers. In heaven, our emotions will be so taken up with the indescribable joy of the union with God that it would be impossible for us to be distracted by anything else. And with our emotional focus set on God in a way that is not subject to distraction, our physical powers will likewise be concentrated on God. Therefore, the bodily expression of love in the marital union of spouses will not occur, for the bodily expression of love will be totally focused on God himself.

3. The Absence of the Marital Union in Heaven

It is very important to understand that the absence of marital union and the marital embrace in heaven is not a deprivation or a lack. In our present state, most of us experience a deep and profound longing to express more adequately our love for God, for our spouses, our children, our friends. A material entity, such as the body, can never fully express a spiritual reality such as a person. The human body, as marvelous as it is, is incapable of completely expressing the movements of the human spirit. Christ's body could not fully express his divine person, and we cannot fully express the movements of the Spirit in us through grace. This would be true even in the state of man before sin, but is even more true for historical man. In heaven, in the resurrection of the body, these limitations of historical man will all pass away, because the divine will penetrate every human power. We will be able to express and feel with our bodily powers the loving union we will have with God much more profoundly than here on earth.

Therefore, we will not experience the absence of the marital union in heaven as a lack. Rather, the very purpose of the marital union, that is, to love one another as God loves us, will be brought to such perfection that we will know and feel that we are totally fulfilled—that we are loving in the way we were created to love. Rather than feeling any loss, we will finally be satisfied that we are adequately expressing our love for God and for others through God. This satisfaction at the adequate expression of love for God—that is, an expression in conformity with our deepest desires—will yield an indescribable joy!

It is obvious from what has been said that the union with God face to face will, strictly speaking, not be a nuptial one if by "nuptial" we mean a union of a man and a woman expressed through the sexual powers. While heaven has been likened to the perfect marriage, this is by way of analogy. "Those who are accounted worthy to attain to that age and to the resurrection from the dead neither marry nor are given in marriage."[14] As John Paul remarks in address 69, "Marriage and procreation in itself do not determine definitively the original and fundamental meaning of being a body or of being, as a body, male and female. Marriage and procreation merely give a concrete reality to that meaning in the dimensions of history. The resurrection indicates the end of the historical dimension."[15] In the resurrection, the full meaning of the human body—that we are created to love—will be fully realized.

4. The Analogy of Earthly Marriage to the Union with God in Heaven Is Inadequate

Given these teachings of Christ, with Pope John Paul's reflections on those teachings, it could be argued that comparing the union of the human person in his or her body/soul unity with God in heaven after the resurrection of the body to marriage runs the risk of serious misunderstanding. Many aspects of earthly marital union are not part of union with God in heaven; for example, the sexual aspects. Thus, there can be a danger in using the marital image for our union with God in heaven. It can mislead people. The image conveys truths of great importance: in heaven we will love God as he loves us; in marriage, spouses are to love each other as God loves us. But we must keep in mind the vast difference between marriage and our relationship with God. In no marriage on earth, even the best, do spouses give themselves to each other in the way God gives himself to us and we will give ourselves to him in heaven.

Even mystical authors who have used marriage as an image to illuminate our relationship with God have been aware of the danger that the image can be misleading. They have pointed out that human words and images are linked to concepts formed from this world. Yet God is so completely *other* that to invoke these concepts and images is to run the risk of conveying falsehoods about him. He is so far beyond human concepts and earthly images as to make them almost lies when applied to him. There is then in mystical thought a long tradition of invoking pure silence with regard to God, knowing that anything we would say is so far beneath the reality as to be more false than true. When comparing the resurrected state of heaven with marriage, it is very good to remember this essential point.

The differences between an earthly marriage and the union with God in heaven are perfectly illustrated by the pope's remark that "the virginal state of the body . . . will be totally manifested as the eschatological fulfillment of the nuptial meaning of the body."[16] In heaven we will all be as virgins; that is, we will not enter into marriage. Still, we will be penetrated by the divine; we will be divinized. We will be taken up into the love of God seen face to face. The nuptial meaning of the body, that is, our recognition that we are called to love as God loves, will be perfectly realized in the total gift of self to God and in his gift of himself to us. And yet, we will not be married. We will be virgins. Both marriage and the virginal state, celibacy and virginity, will find their fulfillment in the union with God.

5. In Heaven We Will Participate in God's Life

The pope writes that the union with God in heaven will be a "concentration of knowledge (vision) and love on God himself—a concentration that cannot be other than full participation in the interior life of God."[17] The word "participation," which is important in the pope's thought, means two or more people uniting to act together in a bond of love while preserving themselves—their own dignity and value—in that union. In a word, participation means joining together with others in love.

For an adequate understanding of John Paul's thought on this point, it is necessary to remember that for the philosopher Karol Wojtyla (later Pope John Paul II), the human person reveals himself through acts. Created as persons, human beings have free will. Unlike the animals, who are programmed by instinct, we have the power of free choice. When we freely choose to act, those acts become part of us and shape us. For example, those who choose to practice playing the piano become piano players. Our acts should always be in conformity with the truth we know through our intellects, and our bodies should be orchestrated by our choices in conformity with the truth. When we freely choose to act in conformity with the truth and our bodies express those acts outwardly, we shape and determine ourselves in a way that transcends the merely physical. Horizontal transcendence occurs when we freely choose our own acts; vertical transcendence occurs when we act in accordance with the truth. Determining and transcending ourselves and acting with integration, that is, with the body expressing what we choose and know to be true, we act as human persons and reveal who we are to the world.

Transcendence, self-determination, and integration are the defining characteristics of human acts. Thus, these characteristics must be present when we act with others. If we are forced to do something against our will, our personal dignity and value are attacked. How do we act together with others in a way that preserves our dignity and value? This is what the pope calls participation. If two or more people, each acting with the characteristics of transcendence, self-determination, and integration, join to do something together, they are participating with one another. As one author puts it, "'Participation' is used by Wojtyla to indicate the way in which, in common acting, the person protects the personalistic value of his own acting and participates together in the realization of common action and its outcomes."[18] "Personalistic value" here refers to the characteristics of transcendence, self-determination, and integration. Participation means not being treated as an object and not treating others as an object; that is, as a mere thing to be used. In fact, in any truly cooperative activity, each person sees the value and dignity of the others and experiences the others affirming that same dignity in himself or herself.

In heaven, participation will reach a level beyond our imagination, because our participation will be with God himself. The Creator himself, who made all of us in his image and likeness, will affirm our dignity and value by giving himself to us so that he will permeate our very being. How could one's dignity and value be more affirmed than by the gift of God himself? Permeated with the divine power, we will also be able to affirm him by giving ourselves to him as he gives himself to us. Of course, God does not in any way need our affirmation. But he loves us so much that we will be able to love and participate with him in the same way that he loves and participates with us. Our affirming of God will be an expansion beyond anything we can imagine of what we do on earth when we praise him for his goodness, for his power, and so on.

In this mutual act of participation, we will experience transcendence, self-determination, and integration to the point that we will become completely who we are meant to be: images of God. We can never reach this goal until we reach heaven, because only in heaven will we be able to love perfectly through transcendence, self-determination, and integration. In other words, only then will we act perfectly as human persons. Our acts will have reached a perfection beyond anything we are capable of in this world. We will reach this perfection only in heaven because only there will we be completely united with him in whose image we are all created.

In this union with God, there is a mutual exchange. Each person receives the gift of the other person and in a certain sense possesses the other person—possesses in the sense of receiving the gift of the other, not in the sense of ownership. All this occurs through the gift of the love of God, and without a loss of self on the part of God or us. God does not absorb us. Rather, he donates himself to us and makes it possible for us to donate ourselves to him. Neither God nor human persons lose their identity or cease to exist, but each comes to possess the other through love, realized through transcendence, self-determination, and integration.

Acting perfectly as human beings, giving ourselves in love to God through the gift of his grace, and receiving God himself in return means a perfect participation with the one to whom we are all drawn because he created us. Only in God can we be satisfied, because only in him, with him, and through him do we "live and move and have our being."[19] Only by receiving his gift of himself in love can our dignity and value as images of him be finally and sufficiently affirmed. Perfected in giving and in receiving, heaven will certainly be "what eye has not seen, and ear has not heard, and what has not entered the human heart."[20]

While everyone in heaven will be individually linked in a communion of persons with God himself in his triune mystery, through God there will be a communion among everyone in heaven. "We must think of the reality of the other world in the categories of the rediscovery of a new, perfect subjectivity of everyone and at the same time of the rediscovery of a new, perfect intersubjectivity of all."[21] Each of us will be totally concentrated on God, and through God, we will be linked to everyone else, because in love, he will possess all of us and, in possessing him through love, we will be united with all others in heaven. This includes those whom we knew on earth. Of course, knowing them in heaven through God is only one of the reasons why we should pray fervently for the salvation of those we love.

D. The Teaching of St. Paul on the Resurrection of the Body: Addresses 70 to 72

In these last three addresses of this cycle, Pope John Paul turns to an analysis of Paul's words regarding the resurrection of the body. In address 70, we read that Paul's perspective is different from Christ's. When Christ answered the question posed to him by the Sadducees, he did not use his own resurrection as an argument for the resurrection of the body, because his own resurrection had not yet happened. But Paul, having seen the risen Christ on the way to Damascus some years after Christ's resurrection, certainly could and did refer to Christ's rising from the dead.

1. The Unity of Creation, the Fall, Redemption, and the Resurrection of the Body

Continuing in address 70, John Paul notes that "Paul studies in depth what Christ had proclaimed. At the same time, he penetrates the various aspects of that truth which had been expressed concisely and substantially in the words written in the synoptic Gospels."[22] For St. Paul, original sin and the plight of historical man point toward the resurrection of the body, just as labor pains in a mother giving birth point to new life. In St. Paul's teaching, there is a unity in God's design between creation, the fall, redemption, and the resurrection of the body.

Address 71 expands on this idea. "The Apostle . . . in a certain way shows two poles between which, in the mystery of creation and redemption, man has been placed in the cosmos. One could say that man has been put in tension between these two poles in the perspective of his eternal destiny regarding, from beginning to end, his human nature itself."[23] John Paul continues, "When Paul writes: 'The first man was from the earth, a man of dust; the second man is from heaven' (1 Corinthians 15:47), he has in mind both Adam and also Christ. Between these two poles—between the first and the second Adam—the process takes place that he expresses in the following words: 'As we have borne the image of the man of earth, so we will bear the image of the man of heaven'

(1 Corinthians 15:49)."[24] We contain within ourselves the Adam of creation and the fall, but also Christ, and we live in the tension between them until the final resolution that occurs through the resurrection of the body. The same teaching is repeated succinctly a little later in address 71: "Every man bears in himself the image of Adam and every man is also called to bear in himself the image of Christ, the image of the risen one."[25]

2. Sown in Dishonor, Raised in Glory

In address 72 John Paul quotes a statement about the human body in St. Paul's First Letter to the Corinthians: "It is sown in dishonor; it is raised in glory. It is sown dishonorable; it is raised glorious. It is sown weak; it is raised powerful. It is sown in weakness; it is raised in power. It is sown a physical body; it is raised a spiritual body. If there is a physical body, there is also a spiritual body."[26] Elaborating on this quotation, the pope is at some pains to show that in Paul's view of the resurrection, the human body will not just be restored to the state of original innocence, that is, to its state before sin, but rather will have a "new fullness."[27] There cannot be simply a return to the state of Adam and Eve before sin, because that would mean that the human race would have no hope of the vision of God. Without the perspective of heaven, of the spiritualization of the body in a new fullness—a state different from that of Adam and Eve before sin—the whole logic of creation, not to mention the redemption, would fall. After all, God made Adam and Eve to share heaven with him. Certainly, Christ's mission could not simply mean that we were to return to that previous state without any hope of seeing God face to face. We are destined for eternity with God in heaven, a perspective far beyond the state of Adam and Eve in original innocence; that is, before sin.

With the remarks on Paul's view of the resurrection of the body, the pope concludes this third cycle of his theology of the body. He also concludes the study of the "words" of Christ on the body/soul relationship in the human person. The next three cycles of the theology of the body will apply the analysis already undertaken to the areas of celibacy and virginity (fourth cycle), marriage (fifth cycle), and the teaching of the church on the connection between the marital embrace and procreation (sixth cycle). Since celibacy and virginity have always been understood by the church as a sign of the future perfection of humanity in heaven after the resurrection of the body, Pope John Paul's analysis of Christ's and Paul's words on the resurrection of the body are fundamental to his examination of celibacy and virginity undertaken in the cycle that follows.

1. See TB, no. 64, p. 233 (1).

2. See Genesis 38:8.

3. See Matthew 22:23-32. See also Mark 12:18-27 and Luke 20:27-38.

4. See Mark 12:25.

5. See TB, no. 66, p. 238 (3).

6. See TB, no. 66, p. 240 (4).

7. See Luke 20:36.

8. See TB, no. 66, p. 240 (5). In this quotation, Pope John Paul II is using an older translation. Compare Douay: "Thou hast made him little less than the angels." The RSV translates Psalm 8:5-6 as "Yet thou hast made him little less than God, and dost crown him with glory and honor. Thou hast given him dominion over the works of thy hands; thou hast put all things under his feet."

9. See TB, no. 67, p. 241 (1).

10. See TB, no. 67, p. 242 (3).

11. See TB, no. 67, p. 242 (4).

12. See TB, no. 67, p. 242 (3).

13. See TB, no. 68, p. 244 (3).

14. See Luke 20:35.

15. See TB, no. 69, p. 247 (4).

16. See TB, no. 68, p. 244 (3).

17. See TB, no. 68, p. 244 (4).

18. See Buttligione, *Karol Wojtyla*, p. 169.

19. See Acts 17:28.

20. See 1 Corinthians 2:9.

21. See TB, no. 68, p. 245 (4).

22. See TB, no. 70, pp. 250–51 (5).

23. See TB, no. 71, p. 253 (2).

24. See TB, no. 71, p. 253 (2).

25. See TB, no. 71, p. 254 (4).

26. See 1 Corinthians 15:42-44.

27. See TB, no. 72, p. 256 (3).

Celibacy
and Virginity

General Audience Addresses 73 to 86

A. INTRODUCTION

The first three cycles of the theology of the body addresses are an analysis of the *existence* of the human person in his or her body/person unity, the principle thesis of which is that the human body is the expression of the person. These three cycles describe the different ways the human body expresses the human person: in paradise before sin (first cycle); after sin but before the resurrection of the body (second cycle); and finally, after the resurrection of the body in heaven (third cycle). The fourth, fifth, and sixth cycles of the theology of the body are an analysis of human *acts*, that is, of the different ways the human body expresses love. In the fourth cycle (addresses 73 to 86), John Paul discusses the bodily expression of love through virginity and celibacy embraced for the sake of the kingdom of God; in the fifth cycle he examines the love of spouses in marriage; and in the sixth cycle he studies the relationship of marriage and procreation.

The topic of virginity or celibacy is a difficult one in the context of the theology of the body, because at first glance it may seem contrary to the way we were created. The pope has established that God created human beings in his image and likeness as persons with bodies. As images of God, human beings are called to do what he does; that is, to love one another as he loves himself in the mystery of the Trinity, and as he loves all created persons. This "innate vocation" of every human being is "inscribed in the humanity of man and woman."[1] Thus, this vocation was clear first to Adam, and then to Eve, and is knowable by every human person born into this world. It is crystal clear to all of us because this meaning is "inscribed" in our very flesh. Our masculinity and femininity are physical signs given to us so that we might know that we are called to enter a loving communion in imitation of the trinitarian communion. This is what John Paul called the nuptial meaning of the body.

Our bodies not only reveal to us that we are to love others as God loves himself and us; they also are the means of expressing or manifesting this love in the world. As we enter loving communions, we express our love in and through our bodies. As human persons we are created by God in a body/person unity so that our acts (at least those that are not purely internal) will be visible. When acting as God acts and expressing those acts outwardly in and through our bodies, we become visible images of God. We are the only beings God has created who can and should be visible images of the Creator himself.

Marriage is, of course, the primary human communion of persons. After creating them "male and female," God called them to imitate his own loving trinitarian communion by inviting Adam and Eve to "be fertile and multiply,"[2] that is, to become the first human married couple. With an eloquence that betrays his love of language in drama and poetry, the pope strikingly describes the incredible blessing and goodness God has conferred on the human race in inviting each of us to imitate his own trinitarian communion through marriage. John Paul's theology of the body, most especially the first two cycles of the series, has one of the most exalted and noble theological word paintings of marriage the church has ever proposed.

Given this exalted description of spousal communion, the whole question of virginity and celibacy for the sake of the kingdom of God takes on a certain urgency. The question is obvious. If marriage is such an exalted calling, willed by the Creator himself, inscribed in the very flesh of every human person, why would anyone choose not to enter into such a communion? And especially, why would anyone choose not to marry for the sake of the kingdom of God? The choice seems almost contradictory to the will of God manifested when he created us male and female and when he said, "It is not good that the man should be alone."[3]

John Paul admits this paradox. Speaking about Christ's words recommending virginity and celibacy for the sake of the kingdom of God,[4] he writes that Christ in a certain sense "expressed himself even in opposition to that beginning to which he himself had appealed."[5] John Paul's reference here to Christ's teaching on the beginning recalls Christ's answer to the Pharisees' question on divorce: "Is it lawful for a man to divorce his wife for any cause whatever?" He said in reply, "Have you not read that he who made them from the beginning made them male and female, and said, 'For this reason a man shall leave his father and mother and be joined to his wife, and the two shall become one'? So they are no longer two but one. What therefore God has joined together, let no man put asunder."[6] It was from this reference to the beginning that John Paul began his analysis of the first pages of Genesis, because, as the pope has taught us, when Christ referred to the beginning, he was saying to the Pharisees that the true nature of marriage is to be derived from the state of the human race before sin. In admitting that Christ's words about virginity and celibacy for the sake of the kingdom of God seem to be in opposition to the beginning, the pope is admitting that virginity and celibacy for the sake of the kingdom seem to be opposed to Christ's own exalted teaching on the beauty of marriage.

On the other hand, Christ's words on virginity and celibacy are just as much part of his teaching as are his words on marriage. In fact, his teaching on virginity and celibacy follows his answer to the Pharisees' question about divorce. Obviously, Christ did not consider his teaching on marriage and his teaching on celibacy and virginity to be contradictory. Therefore, even though there seems to be a paradox, ultimately these two aspects of revelation cannot be in opposition to one another. In fact, there are many paradoxes in the teaching of the Lord—for example, that death to self is a means of living life to the fullest—and there are many more.[7]

Christ's teaching on celibacy and virginity for the sake of the kingdom of God is clearly understood by Pope John Paul II according to the most basic principles of the theology of the body. The essential point of John Paul's analysis of the human body is that it is the expression of the person. In his meditations on the Stations of the Cross, given as part of his retreat preached to Pope Paul VI in 1976, John Paul—then Cardinal Karol Wojtyla—said about Christ at the tenth station, where Christ is stripped of his garments, "With every wound, every spasm of pain, every wrenched muscle, every trickle of blood, with all the exhaustion in its arms, all the bruises and lacerations on its back and shoulders, this unclothed body is carrying out the will of both Father and Son."[8] Christ's body expressed his Person because through his body, his choices—the acts of his will—were expressed or manifested. Clearly, these choices rested on his knowledge in his intellect. Therefore, his body expressed his Person, because through it he manifested and outwardly demonstrated what he was thinking and choosing.

The human body, not just in Christ but in all of us, expresses our persons; that is, makes apparent what we are thinking and choosing. In coming to know another person, a future spouse, a man or woman might first be drawn by beauty or handsomeness, by a sense of charm or strength; in short, by all those characteristics that we associate with masculinity or femininity. But, if this relationship is to rest on a firm foundation, eventually one must come to see the dignity with which that other person was created by God. He or she comes to understand that here is another person who is also an image of God. In coming to understand the dignity and value of the other person, sometimes love develops—a deliberate choice in the will to give oneself to this other person because of the great treasure, the infinite value, of the other person as understood by the mind. When such a choice is met by a similar choice made by the other, there is a mutual commitment, which is then sealed by the marriage vows repeated before a witness of the church. The vows establish the marital communion. The marital communion is then expressed by the union of the two in one flesh. The bodily expression of the communion is the direct result of the spouses' knowledge of each other and their mutual choice to give themselves to one another.

But, just as obviously, we can freely choose not to enter such a communion. If the marital communion rests on the knowledge of the dignity of another and on a free choice to give oneself to that other person, then it is obvious that people are not forced to make such a choice. In fact, force is contrary to love and invalidates marriages. For example, "shotgun" weddings are not recognized, because force is opposed to love, which is, in its essence, a free choice. Every person can choose not to enter into a marital communion. Perhaps an individual is not suited to marry. Another may not yet have met someone appropriate. A third might choose not to marry because he or she desires to remain unmarried.

If the nuptial meaning of the body shows that we are called to love God and others as God loves us and to express that love in and through our bodies, it certainly must be possible to choose to express one's love for Christ and all that he did through his passion and death by loving him without entering the marital communion. Indeed, why couldn't someone imitate Christ in his celibate state? Of course, as the church has taught from the beginning, this way of life is not only possible but praiseworthy for the one who is called to it. As the pope puts it, "Man (male and female) is capable of choosing the personal gift of his very self. This is made to another person in a conjugal pact in which they become 'one flesh.' He is also capable of freely renouncing such a giving of himself to another person, so that, choosing continence 'for the sake of the kingdom of heaven,' he can give himself totally to Christ. On the basis of the same disposition of the personal subject and on the basis of the same nuptial meaning of the being as a body, male or female, there can be formed the love that commits man to marriage for the whole duration of his life (cf. Matthew 19:3-10). But there can also be formed the love that commits man to a life of continence for the sake of the kingdom of heaven (cf. Matthew 19:11-12)."[9]

B. Celibacy and Virginity for the Sake of the Kingdom: Addresses 73 to 76

1. Marriage Is the Ordinary Vocation

Marriage and family life are blessings from God and the normal vocation for men and women. For this reason, Christ first speaks about marriage and only then about celibacy and virginity.[10] John Paul emphasizes this point in address 73: "It is very significant that Christ did not directly link his words on continence for the kingdom of heaven with his foretelling of the 'other world' in which 'they will neither marry nor be given in marriage.'"[11] Celibacy and virginity embraced for the sake of the kingdom of heaven are lived out in the context of this world, of "historical" man. Had Christ linked his remarks on celibacy and virginity to his teaching on the "other world," rather than to his teaching on marriage, then celibacy and virginity for the sake of the kingdom might have been understood as *the* path to heaven. As it is, Christ makes it perfectly clear that virginity and celibacy embraced for the sake of the kingdom of God are an "exception to what is rather a general rule of this life,"[12] that is, marriage. It is granted only to some, who are invited to voluntarily accept it: "Not all men can receive this precept, but only those to whom it is given. . . . He who is able to receive this, let him receive it."[13]

2. The Mystery of Vocation

Here we enter into the mystery of vocation. The gentle action of the grace of the Holy Spirit calls each of us to a specific path to heaven, a particular vocation, whether marriage or celibacy. This is the granting that Christ speaks of. But this gentle stirring of God's grace in our hearts must be received in our wills. In any vocation, there are two aspects: the gift of God and the acceptance on our part. Those called to virginity and celibacy ought to accept this vocation, that is, they ought to choose it wholeheartedly in their wills, just as those called to marriage should choose marriage wholeheartedly in their wills.

3. Celibacy and Virginity Are for the Kingdom of God

The requirement that those embracing celibacy or virginity explicitly choose this state for the sake of the kingdom of heaven distinguishes their path of life from the unmarried state after the resurrection of the body and after the second coming, in heaven, when our souls and bodies will be reunited in the glory of God. The pope writes in address 73, "There is an essential difference between man's state in the resurrection of the body and the voluntary choice of continence for the kingdom of heaven in the earthly life and in the historical state of man fallen and redeemed. The eschatological absence of marriage will be a state, that is, the proper and fundamental mode of existence of human beings, men and women, in their glorified bodies. Continence for the kingdom of heaven, as the fruit of a charismatic choice, is an exception in respect to the other stage, namely, that state in which man 'from the beginning' became and remains a participant during the course of his whole earthly existence."[14]

4. The Reaction of the Apostles

In address 74 the pope discusses the reaction of the apostles to Christ's teaching on virginity and celibacy. Jesus acknowledged that they would find his teaching difficult to accept. In the religious beliefs of the chosen people of the Old Testament, marriage was a sacred and holy state. Marriage and procreation were the means by which God's promise to Abraham to make him "the father of a multitude of nations" would be fulfilled. [15] "In the Old Testament tradition, marriage, as a source of fruitfulness and of procreation in regard to descendants, was a religiously privileged state: and privileged by revelation itself." [16]

This divine approbation of marriage through the covenant with Abraham was built on and expanded the previous divine invitation to the entire human race given in the first chapter of Genesis to "be fruitful and multiply." [17] The apostles held marriage as an exalted state willed by God at the very dawn of creation and specifically endorsed by God for the Jewish people as the means of fulfilling the covenant God made with them through the patriarch Abraham. Christ's endorsement of the unmarried state as a particular commitment to the kingdom of God would have seemed to the apostles to contradict the Old Testament and their entire religious heritage. Of course, this theological status of marriage and procreation was one of the reasons why infertility was seen as a sign of God's displeasure.

The only recognized exceptions to the rule of marriage in the Old Testament were "eunuchs who have been so from birth" and those who "have been made eunuchs by men." To these two exceptions to marriage recognized in the old covenant, Christ adds those who "have made themselves eunuchs for the sake of the kingdom of heaven." [18] The addition of this third exception was a very significant "turning point" in revelation. [19] By it Christ introduced a completely new concept, distinguished from the tradition of the old covenant.

How could the apostles who heard Christ's teaching on virginity and celibacy for the kingdom of God have accepted what Christ taught? To ask this question is to ask a whole series of related questions. How could they have accepted his teaching on the Eucharist, when he taught them that they were to "eat the flesh of the Son of man and drink his blood?" [20] They accepted what Christ said because he was the revelation of the Father, a truth they knew through the gift of the Holy Spirit. Thus, on the question of virginity and celibacy for the sake of the kingdom of God, they accepted what he taught them because he said it and because he lived what he said; he was unmarried. The Lord's testimony and his own celibate life were the basis they had for accepting this teaching.

Yet at first the apostles did not understand Christ's words. They responded to his teaching on divorce with the remark, "If such is the case of a man with his wife, it is not expedient to marry."[21] In their view, even though some marriages are satisfactory, others become intolerable. Thus it would be unwise to enter marriage if divorce were unacceptable. It was at this point that Christ offered his teaching on virginity and celibacy.

The Lord invites those called to virginity and celibacy for the sake of the kingdom of God to live this renunciation of marriage and family life not because family life is hard and could lead to sin—for example, it might lead some people to divorce and remarry—but because it is so good. Only the sacrifice of something truly good can be a meaningful gift to God. I am reminded of the comment of a fifth-grader, "I will give up homework for Lent." He knows it is a joke, and everyone laughs, because to him homework is not a good thing. It is work and is sometimes unpleasant. Sacrificing homework would hardly be a gift to God. Giving up his favorite TV show would be something different, because it is something the fifth-grader perceives as good. The only meaningful sacrifice for the kingdom of God is the sacrifice of something good. We should renounce sin for God, but renouncing sin is not the same as sacrificing. To sacrifice means to make holy. By renouncing sin, we are not giving sin to God, because sin cannot be made holy. Thus, strictly speaking, renouncing sin is not a sacrifice, although we sometimes use the word that way. In sacrifice, we are giving back to God something that is good.

The renunciation, or sacrifice, of marriage for the sake of the kingdom of God only makes sense if marriage is truly good and holy, a significant blessing of God to the human race. In teaching that celibacy and virginity for the sake of the kingdom of God should be embraced by those called to this vocation, Christ implicitly rejected the apostles' conclusion that marriage was to be avoided because it may be difficult or might become the occasion for some to sin through divorce and remarriage.

5. The Marriage of Christ's Parents

In address 75, the pope mentions that there was a further testimony to the goodness of continence for the sake of the kingdom of heaven: the marriage of Mary and Joseph. It was not just the Lord's public life that testified to the goodness of virginity and celibacy; it was his entire life from his conception to his ascension. Jesus was conceived by a virgin who remained a virgin her entire life even though married to a husband, Joseph. And Joseph, even as Mary's husband, lived a celibate life. At first, the apostles did not know this history of Christ's parents, conception, and birth, but as the church came to know the marvelous fruitfulness of Joseph and Mary's celibacy and virginity, it could appreciate Christ's teaching on celibacy and virginity in an entirely new way!

And of course, after the resurrection on the first Easter, the apostles must have heard from Mary the profound truths of the Christmas story. In Mary and Joseph, the nuptial union was realized in a complete gift of each to the other and to God for the sake of the kingdom of heaven. It was through them that the full reality and truth of the kingdom of God was announced, because this was precisely the good news their Son gave to the world. How could celibacy and virginity do more for the kingdom of God? At the same time, in their union at Nazareth, they were as committed to one another in love as any couple could have been. John Paul notes this wonderful mystery when he writes, "The marriage of Mary and Joseph (in which the church honors Joseph as Mary's spouse, and Mary as his spouse), conceals within itself, at the same time, the mystery of the perfect communion of the persons, of the man and the woman in the conjugal pact, and also the mystery of that singular continence for the kingdom of heaven. This continence served, in the history of salvation, the most perfect fruitfulness of the Holy Spirit."[22]

The apparent contradiction between the goodness and fruitfulness of marriage, on the one hand, and celibacy and virginity for the sake of the kingdom of God, on the other, is completely resolved in the marriage of Mary and Joseph. "Mary's divine maternity is also, in a certain sense, a superabundant revelation of that fruitfulness in the Holy Spirit to which man submits his spirit, when he freely chooses continence in the body."[23] The physical fruitfulness through procreation in marriage corresponds to the fruitfulness through the Holy Spirit in virginity and celibacy embraced for the sake of the kingdom of God.

In learning this mystery of Mary and Joseph, sometime after the Lord's resurrection, the church could understand Christ's teaching on celibacy and virginity, given to the apostles before his resurrection, in a much better way. Still, it is to the apostles' credit that without knowledge of the example of Mary and Joseph, they still accepted Christ's teaching on the goodness of virginity and celibacy when embraced for the sake of the kingdom of God.

In address 76 John Paul underlines the teaching of Christ that the vocation of celibacy or virginity for the sake of the kingdom must be chosen by each individual who has received such a vocation. While God calls certain individuals to celibacy, he gives each of them a free choice as to whether to accept or reject the call. Further, it must be chosen for a specific motivation: for the sake of the kingdom of heaven, that is, for supernatural reasons of faith. This choice echoes Mary's *fiat* when the angel Gabriel asked her to be the mother of God: "Let it be to me according to your word."[24] Mary gave her assent without a complete understanding of what was happening. She asked how she was to conceive when she was not married. Gabriel answered by speaking of the Holy Spirit. But Mary, as a child of the Old Testament, would not have completely understood Gabriel's answer. The Trinity was to be revealed by her Son in his public life! Similarly, the celibate or virgin choosing his or her vocation does not completely know the fruitfulness of the Holy Spirit that he or she will enjoy. Neither does he or she know how easy or difficult the way may be. John Paul observes that Jesus "does not even seek to conceal the anguish that such a decision and its enduring consequences can have for a man."[25]

C. The Relationship of Marriage and Celibacy/Virginity: Addresses 77 to 81

There is no contradiction between Christ's teaching on celibacy and virginity and his teaching on marriage. Both rest on the body/person unity of the human being. Both rest on the disposition—the knowing and choosing—of a personal subject toward another: either Christ or a spouse. Both consist in an act of self-donation, an act of love, which is expressed in and through the body. Both rest on the revelation that the human being is called to love and to express that love in and through his or her body. Both are fruitful.

In address 77 the pope denies that Christ diminishes the value of marriage in his teaching regarding celibacy and virginity for the sake of the kingdom. However, John Paul does ask himself whether Christ perhaps suggests "the superiority of continence for the kingdom of heaven"[26] without devaluing marriage. The response is that virginity or celibacy has a greater importance for the sake of the kingdom than marriage does, but in no way does this devalue marriage.

1. Christians Are Not Divided by Marriage and Virginity/Celibacy

In address 78, we see that virginity and celibacy for the sake of the kingdom of God are complementary to the marital vocation. Thus the presence of marriage, on one side, and celibacy or virginity, on the other, does not divide Christians. "Marriage and continence are neither opposed to each other, nor do they divide the human (and Christian) community into two camps," that is, into those who are supposedly "perfect" because of celibacy and virginity and those who are supposedly "imperfect" because of marriage. Rather, "these two basic situations, these two 'states,' in a certain sense explain and complete each other as regards the existence and Christian life of this community."[27] (The reference to "perfect" and "less perfect" echo the heretical teachings of the Cathars, sometimes called the Albigensians.[28])

The church in its teaching has used the term "perfect state" for the way of life of the evangelical counsels of poverty, chastity, and obedience. But this term is not equivalent to the "perfect" and "imperfect" of the Cathars. "Perfection" is measured in a Christian by the degree of charity that he or she exercises. The life plan of the evangelical counsels is called a "state of perfection" because it is designed to lead a person to this perfection. "The evangelical counsels undoubtedly help us to achieve a fuller charity."[29] A person is not more perfect because he or she lives in the state of perfection, that is, in an "institute that bases its life plan on vows of poverty, chastity and obedience."[30] Someone who lives in the world in the married state "can *de facto* reach a superior degree of perfection—whose measure is charity—in comparison to the person who lives in the state of perfection with a lesser degree of charity."[31] For example, a husband and father who lives a Christian life and has reached a high degree of charity toward his wife, children, fellow employees, and so on is more perfect than a priest who is habitually angry with his parishioners and others. Not only celibacy and virginity but also "conjugal love must be marked by that fidelity and that donation to the only Spouse (and also of the fidelity and donation of the Spouse to the only Bride), on which religious profession and priestly celibacy are founded."[32]

2. Marriage and Virginity/Celibacy Are Complementary

The vocation of marriage and the vocation of celibacy and virginity confirm and mutually support one another. Both vocations are expressions of love. Both are rooted in the discovery of the nuptial meaning of the body—the discovery that human beings are called to love in imitation of the Trinity and to express that love in and through their bodies. The celibate or virgin is the signpost of the love all men and women owe to God for all his gifts to us. Celibates and virgins also testify to the true destiny of human persons in their body/soul unity: heaven. Those who are married give witness to the intent of the Creator when he made us "male and female." Families give life to new human persons and, through this cooperation with God's creative act, testify to God's ongoing gift of life and love—which are one reality because life is always included in love. Without the constant reminder of God's gift of life and love, how could celibates and virgins maintain their vocation, which reminds everyone of all God has given us? And, obviously, families look toward the true destiny of humanity, because parents know that their fundamental calling is to help each other and their children come to the glorification of the human person in heaven after the resurrection of the body.

3. May We Refuse a Vocation?

Since every vocation is a gift from God, we cannot simply make up our own. Of course, people try to do this all the time. If called to marriage to a specific person, sometimes people will not cooperate with this grace of God. They may doubt that they are actually called to marriage or to marriage with a specific person. Even though they sense that God is nudging them toward marriage to this person, they may decide not to marry. They may refuse the vocation God has granted.

Usually, in refusing such a gift from God, a person finds his or her path to heaven more difficult. It is not so much that there is only one way to heaven for each of us—for example, that a particular person is suited only for marriage or, more specifically, that there is only one possible spouse for that person. But it seems that God calls us to the best possible vocation suited to our personalities and talents. If we refuse to accept this vocation, then there will always be alternative paths to heaven for us, but they may not be the best possible ones for us.

If there were not more than one possible path for each of us, then a vocation could not be accepted freely. The role of our own human free will, what the pope would call human subjectivity, would not exist if God compelled us to choose the only vocation leading to heaven. But such compulsion by God is inconceivable, because it would be an attack on the dignity of the human person. Constituted as persons by the creative act of God himself, human persons can only act by their own free choice and in light of their own knowledge. God would never violate his own creative act by compelling human persons to act in a certain way. This is why God tolerates the choice to sin. Therefore, there must be more than one possible path to heaven for each of us, although for each of us there is a best vocation.

A vocation to virginity or celibacy for the kingdom of heaven must first be granted by God and then accepted by the individual. It is essential that the motive for accepting virginity and celibacy be the kingdom of heaven, for this vocation is one that serves the kingdom of God on earth, the church. The church, therefore, discerns for itself whether an individual truly is called by God to virginity or celibacy. Sometimes people believe they are stirred by God's grace toward the religious life, when in fact they have not received such a grace. In the best of times, the church gently tries to help individuals who may have made a mistaken judgment about a call to virginity and celibacy. In more difficult times, the church's structures that exist to help discern the action of God's grace with respect to the religious vocation do not function the way they should. In these times, people may be treated harshly—much too harshly—and some may enter religious life who are probably called to a different path.

An essential truth hidden in the mystery of God's calling each of us to a specific vocation is very often overlooked in discussions of the religious life in relation to marriage. We do not choose our own vocation independently of God. We are called, and then we choose to follow or not to follow God's invitation. The best vocation is the primary one that God has invited us to follow. For most, that vocation is marriage.

It is next to impossible, except in the most general sense, to speak of vocations in the abstract. For example, it is not very helpful to claim that this or that vocation is "better" than another. Concretely, what is best for an individual is the vocation God has invited that person to embrace. Ultimately, the judgment of every vocation must be based on what God has granted the individual person and how well that person has responded. As John Paul teaches in address 79, "If anyone chooses marriage, he must choose it just as it was instituted by the Creator 'from the beginning.' He must seek in it those values that correspond to God's plan. If on the other hand anyone decides to pursue continence for the kingdom of heaven, he must seek in it the values proper to such a vocation. In other words, one must act in conformity with his chosen vocation."[33] The best vocation for each of us is the one God grants us first and the one we can most easily embrace and live.

4. Both Marriage and Celibacy/Virginity Are Founded on Masculinity and Femininity

In address 80 the pope affirms strongly that those who embrace the celibate or virginal life for the sake of the kingdom do not in any way renounce their own masculinity or femininity. Rather, as spouses give themselves to one another, so the celibate or virgin makes a self-donation of himself or herself to the Lord. As the pope puts it, "Man (male and female) is capable of choosing the personal gift of his very self. This is made to another person in a conjugal pact in which they become 'one flesh.' He is also capable of freely renouncing such a giving of himself to another person, so that, choosing continence for the sake of the kingdom of heaven, he can give himself totally to Christ. On the basis of the same disposition of the personal subject and on the basis of the same nuptial meaning of the being as a body, male or female, there can be formed the love that commits man to marriage for the whole duration of his life (cf. Mt 19:3-10). But there can also be formed the love that commits man to a life of continence for the sake of the kingdom of heaven (cf. Mt 19:11-12)."[34] Celibates or virgins express their love of Christ in and through their bodies, but in a different way than spouses. Consecrated virgins—religious sisters and those living in the world—express their love of God in a feminine way, both in their work and their spirituality. Their feminine expression of the love of God differs from the masculine expression. Priests and religious brothers have a masculine expression of their love of God that is characterized also in their work and in their spirituality.[35]

In the following address (81) John Paul makes another statement about the complementarity of marriage and celibacy or virginity for the sake of the kingdom of God. To embrace celibacy or virginity for the sake of the kingdom, those called to this vocation must realize what marriage is in all of its goodness. Without this knowledge, their choice of celibacy or virginity would be meaningless. "If continence for the sake of the kingdom of heaven undoubtedly signifies a renunciation, this renunciation is at the same time an affirmation."[36]

D. The Teaching of St. Paul on Virginity/Celibacy: Addresses 82 to 86

In his study of the human person in his or her body/person unity after the resurrection, John Paul first considered the words of Christ in answer to the Sadducees' question and then took up the teaching of St. Paul. Similarly, in this cycle on celibacy and virginity for the sake of the kingdom of God, John Paul concludes with five addresses (82 to 86) on the teaching of St. Paul regarding virginity and celibacy.

1. Paul Writes as a Pastor

In address 82 the pope quotes 1 Corinthians 7:25: "With regard to virgins, I have no command from the Lord, but I give my opinion."[37] Clearly, as the pope notes, St. Paul is distinguishing, as Christ did, between a counsel and a commandment. Further, Paul is speaking in response to questions addressed to him by members of the church at Corinth. The very first lines of the chapter are "Now concerning the matters about which you wrote."[38] He is answering questions about marriage and virginity presented to him, perhaps by a young man who is struggling with the question of whether or not to marry, or by a newlywed, or by the guardian of a young woman. Paul's teaching has to be seen as the response of a pastor to a particular problem. The task then of properly understanding St. Paul's intent in 1 Corinthians 7 is to interpret the doctrinal teaching in light of the personal and pastoral elements. This is the task John Paul has accomplished in the last addresses of the fourth cycle.

It is noted in address 82 that the question posed to the apostle originated in the Greek culture of Corinth. This context was radically different from the Jewish culture of Palestine. The question posed to St. Paul might have originated in ideas circulating in Corinth that marriage was somehow sinful. Such a thought could easily have come from "dualistic pro-gnostic currents, which later become . . . Manichaeism."[39]

Dualism here means the general concept that the material world is evil and the spiritual world is good. Such thinking was prevalent in later Gnostic circles and in Manichaeism. Dualistic thinking looks with disfavor on marriage since marriage obviously involves the body, which is material. St. Paul, as the pope notes, clearly denies that marriage is in any way evil or sinful: "If you marry, you do not sin, and if a girl marries, she does not sin (1 Corinthians 7:27-28)."[40]

In address 83 the pope takes up St. Paul's line "He who marries his betrothed does well; and he who refrains from marriage will do better."[41] The reason Paul gives that those who remain unmarried "will do better" is that "they will have troubles in the flesh, and I would wish to spare them that."[42] By "troubles in the flesh" Paul probably means difficulties of a moral nature. St Paul here reveals the heart of a pastor who has the care of his flock as the motivation for what he does. He wishes to spare his flock as much pain as possible. Commenting on St. Paul's advice, John Paul writes, "In this realistic observation we must see a just warning for those who—as at times young people do—hold that conjugal union and living together must bring them only happiness and joy. The experience of life shows that spouses are not rarely disappointed in what they were greatly expecting."[43] Paul is teaching that marriage demands sacrifice and is not, as the pope notes, an "easy" love. Paul is not saying that marriage is bad!

How many deacons, priests, bishops, even popes, as well as marriage counselors and all those in the helping professions have not had a similar thought from time to time when faced with some of the difficulties presented by their married parishioners or clients? Just because one wants to spare people difficulties in marriage does not mean that one necessarily is against marriage. And clearly, Paul was not against marriage! He talks of a Christian wife or husband consecrating an unbelieving spouse.[44] He speaks of husbands and wives not separating.[45] He states that marriage is not sinful and that it is a call assigned by God. Finally he teaches that those who marry do well!

St. Paul's chief reason for embracing celibacy and virginity for the sake of the kingdom of heaven is that the celibate or virgin is "anxious about the affairs of the Lord" and wants to "please the Lord."[46] In these two remarks, St. Paul clearly highlights the motive for embracing celibacy or virginity for the sake of the kingdom. There are two aspects to this motivation. First, one is concerned about the affairs of the Lord; that is, the kingdom of God. "With this concise expression, Paul embraces the entire objective reality of the kingdom of God."[47] Second, the virgin or celibate wants to "please the Lord." In other words, there is a very special relationship of love for Christ that must be a constitutive part of the motivation of the person embracing celibacy or virginity for the sake of the kingdom. The celibate or virgin must unite his or her will with Christ's as Christ united his will with the Father's and always did "what is pleasing to him."[48]

2. Was Corinth Different from Palestine?

In address 84 John Paul reminds us that in interpreting St. Paul's teaching in the seventh chapter of first Corinthians, we must be mindful that the people in Corinth were gentile converts to Christianity. They were not steeped in the traditional Old Testament Jewish understanding of marriage and procreation. Their understanding of marriage had been shaped by the pagan culture that existed in the Roman Empire at the time of Christ. "Marriage was understood as a way of 'making use of the world'—differently from how it had been in the whole Jewish tradition (despite some perversions, which Jesus pointed out in his conversation with the Pharisees and in his Sermon on the Mount)."[49]

In speaking about marriage and virginity to his Corinthian flock, Paul had not only to hold out the possibility of virginity and celibacy for the sake of the kingdom of God but also to ensure that his followers understood marriage in the proper Christian context. Therefore, Paul stresses the transience of this world. In 1 Corinthians 7:29, he insists that "the appointed time has become very short," because he wants to stress the future world of heaven to which all are called. He repeats this thought in 7:31: "For the form of this world is passing away." To those who had had the practice of enjoying all the pleasures of this world—and marriage was one way of "using the world" in this way—Paul admonishes his readers that this world is not everything, that there is a future world to which all Christians, married or unmarried, are destined. In his pastoral way, Paul is telling his married readers that they need to live marriage differently than their culture would dictate. "Undoubtedly, all this explains the style of Paul's answer. The Apostle is well aware that by encouraging abstinence from marriage, at the same time he had to stress a way of understanding marriage that would be in conformity with the whole evangelical order of values."[50]

3. Vocation as Gift

The Corinthian Christians' misunderstandings about marriage in light of the gospel, as well as the question asked of Paul, give a certain coloring to his response. But the pope reminds us that this pastoral coloring must be read in light of a principle the apostle clearly lays down: "Each has his own special gift from God."[51] In 1 Corinthians 7:17, we read, "Let every one lead the life which the Lord has assigned to him. . . . This is my rule in all the churches." St. Paul teaches this principle as a command. Finally, in 7:20, we hear that "every one should remain in the state in which he was called." In all of these verses, St. Paul is talking about a vocation, a call from God. He is also clearly saying that everyone should follow the vocation given to him or her by God and remain in that vocation. Everything else in Paul's remarks about marriage and virginity or celibacy must be read in light of these "orders" he has laid down.

The major point of address 85 is expressed in the third paragraph: "According to Paul's teaching, the Christian must live marriage from the point of view of his definitive vocation. Marriage is tied in with the form of this world which is passing away and therefore in a certain sense imposes the necessity of being locked in this transiency. . . . For this reason the Apostle declares that the one who chooses continence does better"[52]—but only if one is called to the vocation of continence. "In both the one and the other way of living—today we would say in one and the other vocation—the 'gift' that each one receives from God is operative, that is, the grace that makes the body 'a temple of the Holy Spirit.'"[53]

Finally, in address 86 the pope summarizes his remarks on virginity and celibacy for the sake of the kingdom of heaven. Abstention from marriage is chosen for the sake of the kingdom of heaven, which comes to its fulfillment after the second coming in the reuniting of the soul and body of each individual human person. It is chosen with a view to the end times and the final victory over sin. In light of this goal, "In his daily life man must draw from the mystery of the redemption of the body the inspiration and the strength to overcome the evil that is dormant in him under the form of the threefold concupiscence. Man and woman, bound in marriage, must daily undertake the task of the indissoluble union of that covenant that they have made between them. But also a man or a woman who has voluntarily chosen continence for the sake of the kingdom of heaven must daily give a living witness of fidelity to that choice, heeding the directives of Christ in the Gospel and those of Paul the Apostle in First Corinthians."[54]

E. Conclusion of the Fourth Cycle

In this fourth cycle of the theology of the body (addresses 73 to 86), John Paul has tackled a very difficult and long-standing problem in Catholic moral theology: the relationship between the vocation of marriage and the vocation of celibacy and virginity for the sake of the kingdom of God. His analysis both of Christ's and St. Paul's words, which brilliantly takes into account the personal and concrete circumstances in which those words were said or written, clarifies and solves some thorny theological difficulties. At the same time, the analysis is carried out on the basis of the principles he has already taught in the previous three cycles of the theology of the body. The next cycle will study how human persons love in marriage.

1. See *Familiaris Consortio*, 11.
2. See Genesis 1:28.
3. See Genesis 2:18.
4. See Matthew 19:11-12.
5. See TB, no. 76, p. 272 (5).
6. See Matthew 19:3-6.
7. See TB, no. 81, p. 285 (3).
8. See Wojtyla, *Sign of Contradiction*, p. 192.
9. See TB, no. 80, p. 284 (6).
10. See Matthew 19:3-12.
11. See TB, no. 73, p. 264 (5).
12. See TB, no. 73, p. 264 (5).
13. See Matthew 19:11-12.
14. See TB, no. 73, p. 263 (4).

15. See Genesis 17:4.

16. See TB, no. 74, pp. 265–66 (3).

17. See Genesis 1:28.

18. See Matthew 19:12.

19. See TB, no. 74, p. 266 (4).

20. See John 6:54.

21. See Matthew 19:10.

22. See TB, no. 75, p. 268 (3).

23. See TB, no. 75, p. 269 (3).

24. See Luke 1:38.

25. See TB, no. 76, p. 272 (5).

26. See TB, no. 77, p. 275 (5).

27. See TB, no. 78, p. 276 (2).

28. See TB, no. 78, p. 276 (2). The Cathars were dualistic. They held that there are two gods: a good god who created the spiritual world and an evil one who created the material world. Each human person is to try to free his or her spiritual powers from the evil of the material world, even from one's own body. Those who embrace the renunciation of the material world in a perfect way were the "perfect" in the Cathar heresy. Others were very much considered to be "imperfect." See Richard M. Hogan, *Dissent from the Creed* (Huntington, IN: Our Sunday Visitor, 2001), pp. 171–80.

29. See TB, no. 78, p. 277 (3).

30. See TB, no. 78, p. 277 (3).

31. See TB, no. 78, p. 277 (3).

32. See TB, no. 78, p. 277 (4).

33. See TB, no. 79, p. 280 (6).

34. See TB, no. 80, p. 284 (6).

35. Those who advise both male and female religious orders know this to be true. What are effective strategies in the feminine religious communities often are ineffectual with masculine religious communities and vice versa.

36. See TB, no. 81, p. 286 (6).

37. See TB, no. 82, p. 288 (3).

38. See 1 Corinthians 7:1.

39. See TB, no. 82, p. 289 (6).

40. See TB, no. 82, p. 289 (6).

41. See 1 Corinthians 7:38.

42. See TB, no. 83, p. 290 (2), and 1 Corinthians 7:28.

43. See TB, no. 83, p. 290 (3).

44. See 1 Corinthians 7:14.

45. See 1 Corinthians 7:10-11.

46. See 1 Corinthians 7:32.

47. See TB, no. 83, p. 291 (8).

48. See TB, no. 83, p. 292 (9), and John 8:29. The theme of Christ's always doing the will of the Father, that is, "what is pleasing to him," is prominent in all of John Paul's teaching. See especially *Sign of Contradiction*, p. 192, and in general John Paul's meditations on the Stations of the Cross in chapter 21 of *Sign*, pp. 185–95.

49. See TB, no. 84, p. 294 (6). See also 1 Corinthians 7:31, where Paul advises the Corinthians using the world not to use it fully. The pope makes reference to this phrase in the quotation cited.

50. See TB, no. 84, pp. 294–95 (6).

51. See 1 Corinthians 7:7.

52. See TB, no. 85, p. 296 (2).

53. See TB, no. 85, p. 297 (4).

54. See TB, no. 86, p. 301 (7).

Marriage

General Audience Addresses 87 to 113

A. Introduction

The previous cycle of the theology of the body discussed the question of celibacy and virginity in light of the results of the studies of the human person undertaken in the first three cycles. In those first three cycles, as the reader may remember, the pope discussed the human person in the garden of Eden before sin (first cycle), the human person after sin, that is, historical man, (second cycle), and the human person after the second coming and the resurrection (third cycle). The starting points for the first three cycles were three words of Christ: his teaching that divorce was not allowed in the beginning, that looking lustfully constitutes adultery in the heart, and that after the final resurrection there is no giving and taking in marriage. In each of these three conditions of the human person, the human body manifests, reveals, and expresses the human person, but in different ways. The results of these analyses illuminated the question of virginity and celibacy in the fourth cycle.

The fifth cycle applies the results of the first three cycles to marriage, especially in reference to St. Paul's passage about marriage and the church in Ephesians 5. As John Paul writes, this "passage of Ephesians constitutes almost a crowning of those other concise key words"; that is, the three statements of Christ regarding divorce, adultery in the heart, and marriage in heaven. "The theology of the body has emerged from them along its evangelical lines, simple and at the same time fundamental. In a certain sense it is necessary to presuppose that theology in interpreting the above-mentioned passage of the Letter to the Ephesians."[1]

B. An Overview of Ephesians 5: Addresses 87 to 88

The pope notes that in Ephesians 5, St. Paul speaks of the body both in its concrete reality as masculine and feminine; that is, "in its perennial destiny for union in marriage,"[2] and as an image of the church, the body of Christ. The pope then proposes to examine these two meanings of the human body, most especially in light of Paul's great comparison of marriage and the church.

Ephesians 5 points the way toward an analysis of marriage as a sacrament. However, understanding marriage as a sacrament depends on the theology of the body, because the great principle of the theology of the body—that the body is the expression of the person—is sacramental. A sacrament is a sign that makes visible what is invisible and accomplishes what it signifies. For example, the pouring of water in baptism over a child's head points to a cleansing of the soul and the giving of supernatural life. This sign not only makes visible the hidden reality of God's action on the child's soul, it is also the means by which God gives the gift of divine grace.

The human body is sacramental, because it is the expression of the person. The body makes visible what is hidden in the mystery of the person, and at the same time, as the visible manifestation of the person, the body has experiences that affect and change the person. "Therefore, in some way, even if in the most general way, the body enters the definition of sacrament."[3] Clearly, the body also "enters" theology by the "front door" in that it is the means Christ chose to reveal himself, the Father, and the Holy Spirit to us. In Christ, the body became *par excellence* the visible sign of an invisible reality. Having summarized in address 87 what he proposes to do in this fifth cycle, in address 88 John Paul outlines Ephesians 5 and begins his detailed analysis of Ephesians 5:21-33.

C. "WIVES, BE SUBJECT TO YOUR HUSBANDS": ADDRESSES 89 TO 92

In address 89 the pope takes up one of the most difficult issues of the New Testament for modern culture: St. Paul's admonition to wives to be "subject to your husbands."[4] This admonition also appears in other passages of St. Paul's writings.[5] To many in our era, such language is offensive in the extreme and is thought to be the product of what is called the male-dominated culture of Paul's era. Many would argue that such passages should never again see the light of day, at least not in the liturgy.

But these texts are in fact the inspired word of God. We need to know their meaning. Further, it might be argued that those passages that are most difficult for us to understand and to implement in our lives are precisely the ones we need to try to understand and incorporate into our vocations, because the very difficulty we have with them points to a deficiency in us or our culture.

1. Husbands and Wives Are Called to Reverence One Another

Before his admonition to the wives, St. Paul uses identical language for both husbands and wives. He writes in Ephesians 5:21 that both husbands and wives are to "be subject to one another out of reverence for Christ."[6] Clearly, both husbands and wives are to be subject to one another. Paul's teaching is not just that wives are to defer to their husbands, but that both spouses are to defer to each other. After this general remark, the apostle addresses wives in 5:22 and then husbands in 5:25, instructing husbands to love their wives "as Christ loved the church and gave himself up for her."[7]

"Reverence" for Christ is not a cowering fear but rather an awe-filled respect for holiness. Christ is God the Son made man. In him, God is revealed. In him, God has visited his people. Just as Peter, James, and John were struck almost dumb at the transfiguration, so should we always be awed at the holy mystery of the incarnation. Since each of the spouses in a marriage is "another Christ" (Paul is speaking here of the marriage of the baptized), they should see in one another the mystery of Christ. The only proper attitude toward that mystery is reverence, and therefore, a mutual subordination such as they would give to Christ. "The mystery of Christ, penetrating their hearts, engendering in them that holy 'reverence for Christ' (namely *pietas*), should lead them to 'be subject to one another.'"[8] There can be then no domination by one over the other. Of course, 5:22 must be read in light of the general principle in 5:21.

A further aspect of the explanation occurs when St. Paul writes that husbands should "love their wives."[9] "Love excludes every kind of subjection whereby the wife might become a servant or a slave of the husband, an object of unilateral domination. Love makes the husband simultaneously subject to the wife, and thereby subject to the Lord himself, just as the wife to the husband. The community or unity which they should establish through marriage is constituted by a reciprocal donation of self, which is also a mutual subjection."[10]

2. Love and Obedience

Love is of God. In fact, we name him by this activity because that is what he does. God's love was revealed by Christ, most especially in his passion and death. Analyzing Christ's passion, we can see five elements: (1) Christ made a decision ("not my will but yours be done"); (2) his decision was founded on his knowledge of human dignity (he knew that this dignity could be fulfilled only in heaven and that that fulfillment could occur only through the redemption); (3) Christ decided to give himself (what more could he give than what he gave on the cross?); (4) his gift is permanent (he always is our redeemer who bears the wounds of his death); and (5) his gift is life-giving (it gives us the life of grace).

We are created in God's image to love as he loves. Our love must have these five characteristics, or it is not love. Our love then must be the result of a union of wills. Those who love another say to the other: "I give myself to you. I will what you will. I choose what you choose." Of course, this union of wills between the spouses must be consistent with truth and human dignity. If one spouse chooses something that is objectively untrue and against human dignity, the other spouse must urge a better choice. The gift of self is made in full freedom, because the one who loves *wants* to give himself or herself to the other. If it is not done in full freedom, it is not a gift, and therefore is not love. Coercion has no part in a loving relationship. Husbands and wives, at the time they say their vows at the marriage ceremony, freely and with full knowledge choose to donate themselves to each other. They choose in effect to be "subject" to one another. Therefore, the marital union is one of mutual donation, that is, mutual subjection, in the sense of a free choice to subject themselves to one another.

Another way of expressing the same truth is that husbands and wives have chosen in full freedom to obey one another. Obedience is often understood in our culture as what good little children do. Children are obedient who do what their parents ask when the parents ask them to do it; for example, they go to bed when they are told. But this is not the obedience of the gospel, because the children who obey, if they are little, that is, under the age of reason, have not yet learned to love; they do not yet make their own choices in full freedom, with the knowledge necessary for such a choice. They are not consciously giving themselves in a self-donation to their parents. Such mature behavior is beyond them. But if they learn and imitate their parents' love and affection, then gradually, as they mature, they will be able to truly obey, that is, to respond to another because they have given themselves to that person in love. If they do not obey in the sense of the gospel, what are they doing? They are responding out of a sense of trust that the parents have their best interests at heart, because the parents have always taken care of them—or, in some cases, unfortunately, simply out of fear.

Since as a society we have the sense that obedience means what good little children do, it is often considered offensive to ask adults to obey. But it is our limited sense of obedience that is the problem. For husbands and wives to obey, or submit to, one another should not seem offensive to either. Doing so is only doing what they promised to do when they said their marriage vows: to love each other by giving themselves freely to each other in a union of wills; that is, to choose in full freedom to do what the other wills. Even obedience toward the precepts of God must be preceded by love. St. Augustine asked, "Does love bring about the keeping of the commandments, or does the keeping of the commandments bring about love?" His response was, "Who can doubt that love comes first? For the one who does not love has no reason for keeping the commandments."[11]

Without love, without a mutual self-donation, that is, mutual union of wills, doing the bidding of another would be unworthy of a human person. Machines and animals do what we will, but they have no choice, no free will. We dare not offend human dignity and value by reducing another to an object, a thing, a machine or an animal, which does not possess the power of choosing. Human dignity and value rest on the foundation of human personhood, and the powers that make us persons are our minds and wills. If a human person, sufficiently mature to use the powers of mind and will, is to act in accord with his or her very being, with his or her dignity, he or she must *choose* to do what another asks before he or she does it. This choice must be founded on some knowledge, even if it is a reliance on the knowledge of the one who gives the command, for example, a superior officer who asks this or that of me for the good of the country. But we dare not, cannot, ask others simply to do our bidding without granting them the dignity of choosing on the basis of some knowledge. For the gift of spouses in marriage, the knowledge is the knowledge that they each have of their own dignity and that of the spouse. The choice is to give themselves to each other in a mutual self donation. It is permanent and life-giving. In other words, marriage mirrors the love of Christ with its five characteristics.

In this context, marriage involves a mutual subjection, a mutual obedience. Clearly, this is Paul's intent, because he asks both husbands and wives to "reverence" one another. He then specifies that wives should love their husbands and husbands should love their wives. These admonitions are founded on the entire Bible, especially on the reality of marriage as created by the Father "in the beginning."

3. St. Paul's Comparison of Marriage and the Church

After commenting on the question of mutual subjection and obedience, in address 89 John Paul takes up the "great analogy" between marriage and the church that Paul sketches in Ephesians 5:22-25: "Wives, be subject to your husbands, as to the Lord. For the husband is the head of the wife as Christ is the head of the church, his body, and is himself its Savior. As the church is subject to Christ, so let wives also be subject in everything to their husbands. Husbands, love your wives, as Christ loved the church and gave himself up for her." There are four components in Paul's analogy: wives, husbands, Christ, and the church. Wives are supposed to have a relationship with their husbands as the church has with Christ.

Christ is compared to husbands and the church is compared to wives. It is vital to notice that Paul is not only saying that the Christ-church relationship is like marriage; he is also saying that marriage is like the relationship between Christ and the church. This second element—viewing marriage in terms of the Christ-church relationship—is a very important part of the great analogy. It is also important to notice that the spousal analogy for the relationship of Christ to the church exists in St. Paul's treatment simultaneously with the analogy of the church as the body of Christ, since St. Paul speaks of Christ as the "head" of the church. "It seems," John Paul observes, that the spousal analogy of the relationship between Christ and the church "serves as a complement to that of the Mystical Body."[12]

Thus, the comparison of marriage to the relationship of Christ to the church moves in both directions. In other words, marriage is illumined and better understood through the relationship of Christ to the church, and the relationship of Christ to the church can be better understood through marriage. John Paul insists in address 90 that the focus of the analogy of Ephesians 5 moves from the Christ-church relationship to the husband-wife relationship. "The call which the author of Ephesians directed to the spouses" is that "they model their reciprocal relationship on the relationship of Christ to the Church."[13] In address 91 the pope reemphasizes the point that the analogy must be read in this direction: Christ's love "is an image and above all a model of the love which the husband should show to his wife in marriage, when the two are subject to each other 'out of reverence for Christ.'"[14] Most often, Paul's words have been read as teaching that the church's relationship with Christ was illumined by the husband-wife relationship. Therefore, John Paul's teaching on this matter provides a vital complement.

4. Husband and Wife Are "One Flesh"

In address 92 we read the familiar line that in marriage the spouses "become one flesh." St. Paul acknowledges the "one flesh" aspect of marriage when he speaks of the husband as the head of the wife. The same aspect is applied to Christ who is "head of the church." Just as the church is "one body" with Christ because the church is the mystical body of Christ, so spouses are "one body" with each another. The "one flesh, one body" of Christ and the church parallels the "one flesh, one body" of spouses. In fact, spouses are to strive to become "one body" as Christ and the church are "one body." This truth is another way in which the analogy in Ephesians moves from the church to spouses, and not exclusively in the other direction. But Christ is also a "husband." Therefore, these two characteristics—being one body and being bride and bridegroom—must always be kept in mind when studying St. Paul's analogy.

Continuing in address 92, we read that "in a certain sense, love makes the 'I' of the other person his own 'I': the 'I' of the wife, I would say, becomes through love the 'I' of the husband. The body is the expression of that 'I' and the foundation of its identity. . . . Being the object of the spousal love of the husband, the wife becomes 'one flesh' with him, in a certain sense, his own flesh."[15] In a startling insight, the pope even suggests that "the wife's submission to her husband . . . signifies above all the 'experiencing of love.'"[16] The unique experience of love in marriage is the conjugal embrace. Obviously, if this interpretation is accepted, the submission of the wife is even more the result of the commitment of love made in the marriage vows!

"Husbands should love their wives as their own bodies. He who loves his wife loves himself. For no man ever hates his own flesh, but nourishes and cherishes it, as Christ does the church" (Ephesians 5:28-29). In this passage, of course, St. Paul again emphasizes the one-flesh union, but in this context, the emphasis is on how the husband is to care for "his own flesh," that is, the body of his wife. Toward the end of this address, the pope tells us that these lines help us "to understand, at least in a general way, the dignity of the body and the moral imperative to care for its good."[17] In the one flesh union of marriage, love is expressed in part by care for the spouse's body; indeed, each spouse cares for the other's flesh as if it were his or her own. Such a concept is hardly domination of the wife by the husband or, still less, the subordination of the wife to the husband.

D. CHRIST'S LOVE OF THE CHURCH: ADDRESS 93 TO 96

After the emphasis on the care of the body, St. Paul quotes Genesis 2:24: "For this reason a man shall leave his father and mother and be joined to his wife, and the two shall become one flesh."[18] This statement, following the previous verses and their obvious meaning, establishes a definitive link between the marriage of Adam and Eve and the relationship of Christ and the church. In address 93, the pope makes this point very clearly. By quoting Genesis 2:24, he says, "the author of the Letter to the Ephesians sums up . . . all that he had said previously, tracing the analogy and presenting the similarity between the unity of the spouses and the unity of Christ with the Church."[19]

1. The Basis of Paul's Comparison of Marriage with Christ and the Church

The fundamental basis for the analogy of marriage to Christ and the church is that marriage is "the most ancient revelation (manifestation)" of God's salvific plan in the created world and Christ is the "definitive revelation and manifestation" of that plan.[20] "This continuity of God's salvific initiative constitutes the essential basis of the great analogy contained in the Letter to the Ephesians."[21]

God manifested himself through Adam and Eve individually, since they were each images of God, and through their marriage, in which they were a reflection of the Trinity. God completed this revelation in Christ, who is also "married" to the church. Still, we can never lose sight of the other image of the church also taught by St. Paul, that Christ and the church form one mystical body, that is, one mystical person.[22]

2. Why It Is Possible to Refer to Christ as Spouse of the Church

In address 94 John Paul insists that just as spouses grant a gift, that is, their very persons, to each other, so Christ, as a spouse, confers on us not only the revelation of the truths about God and ourselves but the graces necessary to live according to those truths. "In him . . . humanity has been chosen 'before the creation of the world,' chosen in love and predestined to the adoption of sons. . . . This supernatural conferring of the fruits of redemption accomplished by Christ acquires the character of a spousal donation of Christ himself to the Church."[23] Christ's love is spousal because he is the definitive revelation of the Father and because he gives his very person to the church in a way analogous to the self-giving of spouses. With the gift of his person to the church, he confers the fruits of his redemption, that is, grace.

In the latter half of address 94 and continuing in 95, the pope reminds us that the image of the marriage of Christ and the church in Ephesians reflects an analogy already expressed in Isaiah: "Your Maker is your husband, the LORD of hosts is his name; and the Holy One of Israel is your Redeemer, the God of the whole earth he is called. For the LORD has called you like a wife forsaken and grieved in spirit, like a wife of youth when she is cast off, says your God. For a brief moment I forsook you, but with great compassion I will gather you."[24]

3. Spousal Love Means Giving through a Human Body

In this passage, God refers to Israel as wife and himself as husband. However, in address 95 John Paul states that "the analogy of spousal love and of marriage appears only when the Creator and the Holy One of Israel of the text of Isaiah is manifested as Redeemer."[25] The Redeemer, as revealed by the New Testament, is Christ. John Paul notes that the beginning of St. Paul's Letter to the Ephesians speaks of God's love for humanity in a paternal way: the Father "has blessed us in Christ with every spiritual blessing in the heavenly places."[26] However, in Christ, in the redeemer, God's love is not so much paternal as spousal, because that love is revealed in and through a human body, in and through Christ's body.

For John Paul, as he explains in addresses 94 and 95, the spousal quality of God's love means that salvific love and revelation occur through a human body. Just as Adam and Eve revealed something of God's love, so in the incarnate Son we see God's love revealed in the flesh. Thus God's paternal love is in a way transformed and completed by the spousal love of Christ—which is spousal because it is revealed in and through a human body. In the full understanding of the Trinity revealed in the New Testament, the image of Isaiah is deepened and made clearer. Only in Christ the redeemer can the spousal love of God be seen clearly because only in Christ does God have a body! Christ makes visible what was in hidden in God. His body is a sign revealing the invisible, just as were the bodies of Adam and Eve.

4. An Adequate Comparison in One Direction, but Not in the Other

Address 96 reminds us that St. Paul's analogy moves in both directions. However, marriage as an analogy for the union of Christ and the church does not sufficiently enlighten us about the mystery of Christ and the church, because the analogy of human spousal love "cannot provide an adequate and complete understanding of that absolutely transcendent Reality which is the divine mystery, both as hidden for ages in God, and in its historical fulfillment in time, when 'Christ so loved the Church and gave himself up for her.'"[27] On the other hand, "the comparison of marriage . . . to the relationship . . . of Christ-Church in the new covenant decides, at the same time, the manner of understanding marriage itself and determines this manner."[28]

E. Marriage as the Primordial Sacrament: Addresses 97 to 99

John Paul calls marriage the primordial sacrament, "understood as a sign which effectively transmits in the visible world the invisible mystery hidden from eternity in God."[29] At the dawn of creation, marriage was a sacrament in the sense quoted here—not yet one of the seven sacraments—because in the marriage of Adam and Eve the love of the Trinity, hidden for all ages in the mystery of the Godhead, was made really, if imperfectly, visible. Further, Adam and Eve were holy and blessed with grace, "an endowment which was the fruit of man's election in Christ before the ages . . . anticipating chronologically his coming in the body."[30] The primordial sacrament was a sign of an invisible reality—a sign that contained holiness, or grace.[31]

Since the primordial sacrament of marriage was a visible sign of a hidden reality with holiness and grace from Christ, it certainly was a prototype of the sacraments of the new covenant. But when "the heritage of original grace, given by God," was dimmed by original sin, marriage "was deprived of that supernatural efficacy which at the moment of its institution belonged to the sacrament of creation in its totality."[32] So we needed a redeemer. "To the marriage of the first husband and wife, as a sign of the supernatural gracing of man in the sacrament of creation, there corresponds the marriage, or rather the analogy of the marriage, of Christ with the Church, as the fundamental great sign of the supernatural gracing of man in the sacrament of redemption."[33] Thus, John Paul concludes, "The mystery hidden in God from all eternity—the mystery that in the beginning, in the sacrament of creation, became a visible reality through the union of the first man and woman in the perspective of marriage—becomes in the sacrament of redemption a visible reality of the indissoluble union of Christ with the Church, which the author of the Letter to the Ephesians presents as the nuptial union of spouses, husband and wife."[34]

In Adam and Eve's marriage, there was the action of Christ—holiness or grace—and the making visible of what was invisible. In the sacrament of redemption, there is the action of Christ—holiness or grace—and the making visible of what was invisible. Since each of the seven sacraments of the church has the action of Christ, conferring holiness or grace, and makes visible what is invisible, they all rest on the primordial sacrament. "One would have to conclude that in a certain sense all the sacraments of the new covenant find their prototype in marriage as the primordial sacrament."[35]

F. Marriage as a Sacrament of the New Covenant: Addresses 100 to 108

But marriage is now also one of the seven sacraments, because Christ has raised this blessing "not forfeited by original sin"[36] to the level of one of the seven sacraments in order to make it possible for all human beings to live marriage in the way it was from the beginning.

1. The Sacrament of Marriage Gives Grace

In address 100 John Paul remarks that, in Ephesians 5, Paul speaks indirectly of the sacraments of baptism and the Eucharist but not of the sacrament of marriage, except as that sacrament is contained in the analogy of marriage to the relationship of Christ to the church. For an examination of marriage as a sacrament, the pope turns to the gospels.

Address 101 contains the argument that after sin it became almost impossible to live marriage according to the original intent of the Creator before sin. But Christ has redeemed us and raised marriage to one of the seven sacraments, restoring the realistic possibility for men and women to live marriage as was originally intended. Through the grace of the sacrament, the command of Christ not to commit adultery can be lived to its fullest. In the Sermon on the Mount, Christ "assigns as a duty to every man the dignity of every woman. Simultaneously . . . he also assigns to every woman the dignity of every man. Finally he assigns to everyone— both to man and woman—their own dignity, in a certain sense, the *sacrum* of the person."[37] The *sacrum* is the sacred, and the sacred is mystery. John Paul here means that every person is a mystery and that each of us has a responsibility to realize that mystery in ourselves as much as we can and to protect it. Husbands and wives have the obligation of protecting each other's *sacrum*. Through the graces given in the sacrament of marriage, it is possible for spouses to make a sincere gift of themselves to each other and not to take one another, that is, not to live on the basis of lust.

The same point is made and emphasized in address 102. "As much as concupiscence darkens the horizon of the inward vision and deprives the heart of the clarity of desires and aspirations, so much does 'life according to the Spirit' (that is, the grace of the sacrament of marriage) permit man and woman to find again the true liberty of the gift, united to the awareness of the spousal meaning of the body in its masculinity and femininity."[38] Further, the pope reminds us, marriage is permanent, indissoluble, and procreative. These characteristics of marriage can be lived through the graces of the sacrament. Above all, we should realize that marriage is a vocation, a path to heaven for spouses. Of particular interest is what John Paul says about *how* marriage helps spouses toward heaven. He says that "marriage is the meeting place of eros with ethos and of their mutual compenetration in the heart of man and of woman."[39] This remark suggests the dynamics by which marriage can help spouses move forward in a process of profound personal transformation. Thus husbands and wives live in the hope of the fulfillment of the redemption through the resurrection of their bodies and the gift of everlasting life with God in heaven.

2. Marriage in Salvation History

In address 103 John Paul sketches God's work through marriage. It was established in creation as the primordial sacrament, as we have seen. It was renewed and restored by Christ through his redemption. It points to heaven because the spousal union of husband and wife has become the means of their personal redemption. Further, marriage is fully lived in heaven after the resurrection, because the spousal gift of love on earth is completely fulfilled in the total gift, including the gift of the body, of all those in heaven to God.

3. The Sacramental Sign of Marriage

In address 104 we read that the sign of the sacrament of marriage is constituted by the intention of the spouses, indicated by their vows, to give themselves to each other in and through their masculinity and femininity. The material element of the sacrament of marriage is the bodies of the two spouses, their masculinity and femininity. Only a man and a woman can give themselves to each other according the language of their bodies. (For this reason, a marriage between two men or two women is impossible.)

In address 105 the pope reminds us that through their masculinity and femininity spouses speak a language—the language of mutual self-donation. If this language is expressing truth—if they truly give themselves to one another in and through their bodies—the husband and wife are living out the sacrament: their bodies become the visible sign of an interior reality. If the language of their bodies expresses a falsehood, they are lying. Adultery is one example of lying with the body. In an adulterous act, one or the other of the spouses tries to "speak" a self-donation through his or her body with someone who is not his or her spouse. Conjugal fidelity is truth, and adultery is nontruth, "a falsity of the language of the body. . . . We can then say that the essential element for marriage as a sacrament is the language of the body in its aspects of truth. Precisely by means of that, the sacramental sign is constituted."[40]

4. Spouses Should Speak the Truth with Their Bodies

Spouses can speak prophetically with their bodies, the pope declares in address 106. When spouses speak the truth of love in and through their bodies, they express what they have chosen in their wills. This choice is founded on the knowledge that, as images of God, they are called to love as God loves and express that love in and through their bodies. They read the call to love in their bodies, in their masculinity and femininity, and decide to act in conformity with this language. As images of God, when they speak the truth with their bodies, they reveal something of God. In fact, when they reread the truth of their bodies and speak that truth to each other, their action takes on a prophetic character. They act as prophets, because a prophet is someone who speaks the truth. When they act in accord with the truth of their bodies, "the language of the body . . . confers, *per se*, a prophetic character"[41] on spousal love.

In address 107 John Paul adds that while the language that the body is capable of speaking is given by God in creation, individual spouses in their own marriage make this language their own. Just as French or German are both existing languages with words and grammar, yet each speaker makes the language his or hers by the words and phrases chosen, so each couple makes use of the language of the body in their own personal ways, while always—to continue the analogy—respecting the grammar and vocabulary of the language of the body.

In the conclusion to this section on marriage as a sacrament (address 108), the pope reiterates that the man of concupiscence, that is, historical man, is capable of rereading the language of the body in truth and can determine his own actions by his knowledge and choice. We are not subject completely to the tendencies toward sin but can, with the help of grace given in the sacrament of marriage, speak the truth with our bodies. "Man, in a real way, is the author of the meanings whereby, after having reread in truth the language of the body, he is also capable of forming in truth that language in the conjugal and family communion of the persons."[42]

G. The Song of Songs and the Book of Tobit: Addresses 109 to 113

After a pause of over fifteen months occasioned by the 1983 Holy Year of the Redemption, John Paul continued the fifth cycle of the theology of the body series on May 23, 1984. In addresses 109 to 111 he comments on the Song of Songs. In address 112 he takes up the story of Sarah and Tobiah in the book of Tobit. Address 113 constitutes the conclusion of the fifth cycle. John Paul writes at the beginning of address 109, "What I intend to explain in the coming weeks constitutes the crowning of what I have illustrated."[43]

1. The Song of Songs

In the three addresses on the Song of Songs John Paul uses all of his poetic and dramatic skill (and, of course, John Paul was an accomplished poet and playwright) to demonstrate that the bride and the groom in the Song of Songs are depicted as they speak the language of the body according to the truth of their mutual love. In address 109 he writes that the bride in the Song of Songs speaks to the groom "through every feminine trait, giving rise to that state of mind that can be defined as fascination, enchantment. This female 'I' is expressed almost without words. Nevertheless, the language of the body, expressed wordlessly, finds a rich echo in the groom's words, in his speaking that is full of poetic transport and metaphors, which attest to the experience of beauty, a love of satisfaction."[44]

Address 110 points out that the bride and the groom in the Song of Songs are responding to a set of values—the values pertaining to human personhood in all the truth of an individual's masculinity or femininity. The values the bride and groom see in one another are constituted not just by their bodies but by their personhood. Each responds to the person revealed in and through the body.

The groom calls his beloved, "sister," a term that connotes a shared history, as though both were of the same family. "Through the name 'sister,' the groom's words tend to reproduce, I would say, the history of the femininity of the person loved. They see her still in the time of girlhood and they embrace her entire 'I,' soul and body, with a disinterested tenderness."[45] The term "sister" also connotes a certain responsibility that both have for one another. This responsibility to a sister or brother reminds us that the pope has previously taught that spouses have entrusted their entire beings to one another and that the human dignity of each is in a certain sense assigned as a responsibility to the spouse. Each spouse is to insure that the dignity of the other is not violated or harmed, most particularly in their marital life.

In an interesting interpretation of the words "A garden locked is my sister, my bride, a garden locked, a fountain sealed,"[46] the pope sees an affirmation that the bride is "master of her own mystery." "The language of the body reread in truth keeps pace with the discovery of the interior inviolability of the person."[47] Even in the intimate belonging of spouses, the individual person remains, because at his or her deepest point, the person is always incommunicable. Although ·spouses belong to one another through their mutual self-donation, their own personhood never disappears in the other. Their own individual mysteries as images of God always remain.

The inviolability of the person leads to a continual and constant mutual discovery and rediscovery. If there were not always something undiscovered or new, something fascinating about the other, in other words, if everything about the other could be known and possessed in the first week or year, marriage would be agony. But even after decades, spouses still discover and rediscover each other, because each of them cannot help but retain his or her own personhood, which can never be fully communicated. John Paul reiterates this point in address 111, when he writes that in the dynamic of love painted in the Song of Songs, there is indirectly revealed "the near impossibility of one person's being appropriated and mastered by the other. The person is someone who surpasses all measures of appropriation and domination, of possession and gratification."[48]

Since the language of the body spoken in the Song of Songs seems, on the one hand, to tend toward possession but also, on the other hand, recognizes the impossibility of such possession, there is a tension not entirely resolved in this text. However, the resolution of the tension is found in St. Paul's words about love: "Love is patient and kind; love is not jealous or boastful; it is not arrogant or rude. Love does not insist on its own way; it is not irritable or resentful; it does not rejoice at wrong, but rejoices in the right. Love bears all things, believes all things, hopes all things, endures all things. Love never ends; as for prophecies, they will pass away; as for tongues, they will cease; as for knowledge, it will pass away."[49] The nature of love sketched by St. Paul knows nothing of possession! The love Paul describes "seems to emerge from another dimension of the person. . . . This love has been called 'agape'."[50] Simply put, grace overcomes any selfish possession.

If the language of the body is to be spoken in truth, then romantic love (the pope uses the term *eros*) must be taken up into the selfless love that was clearly revealed to us by Christ. Only in that refined love, characterized by purity, can the assignment of the dignity of each spouse to the other be fulfilled, because only in that selfless love is there never an attempt at selfish possession.

2. The Book of Tobit

This assignment of each spouse's dignity as a person to the other means that love has objective requirements that each lover must subjectively embrace. As the pope observes, love is as stern as death.[51] This point is explicitly made in the book of Tobit, in which a young man named Tobiah faces death on his wedding night.

Address 112 analyzes the marriage of Tobiah and Sarah. Sarah had been wed seven times, but all seven bridegrooms died on the wedding night before consummating the marriage with her. Therefore, before speaking the language of the body in the marital embrace, Tobiah and Sarah ask God's blessing on their union. They pray together. "They see with the glance of faith the sanctity of this vocation in which—through the unity of the two, built upon the mutual truth of the language of the body—they must respond to the call of God himself."[52] There is an objective content of love that must be spoken by spouses. Otherwise the language of the body does not correspond to the truth of the dignity of the spouses. Further, this objective content is set by God himself. Of course, the spouses must make this objective content part of each of their subjective attitudes toward themselves and one another. In other words, the romantic aspects of the language of the body revealed in the Song of Songs must be merged with the objective truths of human dignity in each of the spouses' attitudes toward themselves and the other.

H. CONCLUSION OF THE FIFTH CYCLE

In the final address of this fifth cycle, John Paul integrates Paul's vision of marriage in Ephesians 5 with his analysis of the Song of Songs and Tobit. He also links both of these Old Testament works with the sacrament of marriage as a renewal of the sacrament of creation. The liturgical language of the sacrament of marriage "assigns to both, to the man and to the woman, love, fidelity and conjugal honesty through the language of the body. It assigns them the unity and the indissolubility of marriage in the language of the body. It assigns them as a duty all the *sacrum* (holy) of the person."[53] The holiness and mystery of each person is the result of God's creative action, because each of us is created in the image and likeness of God. Each of us reflects an infinitesimal aspect of the mystery of God himself. Each of us is an image of God, a "spark of the divine." "The 'language of the body,' as an uninterrupted continuity of liturgical language, is expressed not only as the attraction and mutual pleasure of the Song of Songs, but also as a profound experience of the *sacrum* (the holy). This seems to be infused in the very masculinity and femininity through the dimension of the *mysterium* (mystery), the *mysterium magnum* of the Letter to the Ephesians. This mystery sinks its roots precisely in the beginning, that is, in the mystery of the creation of man, male and female, in the image of God, called from the beginning to be the visible sign of God's creative love."[54] The language of the body is liturgical because liturgy is the language of sacraments. The language of the body is the language of the sacrament of the body in the generic sense, that is, in the sense of the body's capability of making visible what has been hidden for all eternity in God. Thus, the pope can teach that the language of the body is an "uninterrupted continuity of liturgical language." This language of the body, the language of the sacrament of the body, is spoken by the spouses in the Song of Songs.

But in order for spouses to speak the language of the body in truth, the dignity and value of both of them must be incorporated into the language spoken individually by their bodies. They need to be purified from the effects of sin, from concupiscence. They are made able to speak the language of the body in truth, affirming in their mutual mysteries the great mystery of the letter to the Ephesians, through the gift of grace given in the sacrament of matrimony.

As one can see, although the pope's conclusion to his fifth cycle of the theology of the body is set in prose, it is almost poetry. The word painting is more descriptive than discursive. Yet, we grasp his main line of thought. There can be no doubt that the church has never given such a vision of marriage. The union of romance and true love in the language of the body, essential to marriage, is a call to all spouses to live their marriages as Adam and Eve lived theirs before sin. Spouses are asked by the pope to make the objective content of love part of their subjective speaking of the language of the body, and so to express truth through their bodies. Part of this truth is that life is always part of love. Since the life-giving characteristic of love is under attack in our culture, the pope devotes the last cycle, the sixth one, to this characteristic of the truth of love.

1. See TB, no. 87, p. 304 (2).

2. See TB, no. 87, p. 305 (3).

3. See TB, no. 87, p. 305 (5).

4. See Ephesians 5:22.

5. See Colossians 3:18.

6. See Ephesians 5:21.

7. See Ephesians 5:25.

8. See TB, no. 89, p. 309 (2).

9. See Ephesians 5:25 and 28.

10. See TB, no. 89, p. 310 (4).

11. See *Veritatis Splendor*, 22, where the pope cites the pertinent passage from St. Augustine.

12. See TB, no. 90, p. 312 (1).

13. See TB, no. 90, p. 313 (3).

14. See TB, no. 91, p. 316 (4).

15. See TB, no. 92, pp. 319–20 (6).

16. See TB, no. 92, p. 320 (6).

17. See TB, no. 92, p. 321 (8).

18. See Ephesians 5:31.

19. See TB, no. 93, p. 321 (1).

20. See TB, no. 93, pp. 321–22 (1).

21. See TB, no. 93, p. 322 (3).

22. Pius XII in his encyclical, *Mystici Corporis*, June 29, 1943, 66, taught that the church and Christ "form but one mystical person." When St. Paul uses the term "body," he intends to indicate a living, human body. A living, human body is the expression of a person. If the church is the body of Christ, it is also his person. See Hogan and LeVoir, *Faith for Today*, p. 154.

23. See TB, no. 94, p. 325 (5).

24. See Isaiah 54:4-10.

25. See TB, no. 95, p. 329 (6).

26. See Ephesians 1:3.

27. See TB, no. 96, p. 330 (1).

28. See TB, no. 96, p. 332 (5).

29. See TB, no. 97, p. 333 (1).

30. See TB, no. 97, p. 335 (5).

31. It should be noted that in the passage just quoted, John Paul is clearly teaching that God the Son would have become incarnate even without sin. Adam and Eve were "elected," had holiness and grace, when they were created, and this endowment "anticipated" Christ's coming in a body. Having created human beings in his image and likeness, God would have had to will the incarnation, because without the incarnation, how could the human images of God (angels are also images of God but without bodies) have come to know who they were or how they should act? See *Faith for Today*, p. 114. The incarnation was willed the moment God created Adam and Eve. Would Christ have redeemed us without sin? No. But he would have come to "reveal man to man himself." See *Gaudium et Spes*, 22.

32. See TB, no. 98, p. 336 (1).

33. See TB, no. 98, p. 337 (2).

34. See TB, no. 98, p. 338 (4).

35. See TB, no. 99, p. 339 (2).

36. See *Sacramentary*, p. 843.

37. See TB, no. 101, p. 346 (6).

38. See TB, no. 102, p. 349 (5).

39. See TB, no. 102, p. 348 (3).

40. See TB, no. 105, p. 360 (9).

41. See TB, no. 106, p. 362 (5).

42. See TB, no. 108, p. 367 (4).

43. See TB, no. 109, p. 368 (1).

44. See TB, no. 109, p. 370 (4).

45. See TB, no. 110, p. 371 (3).

46. See Song of Songs 4:12.

47. See TB, no. 110, p. 372 (4).

48. See TB, no. 111, p. 374 (3).

49. See 1 Corinthians 13:4-8.

50. See TB, no. 111, p. 375 (3).

51. See Song of Songs 7:6.

52. See TB, no. 112, p. 377 (4).

53. See TB, no. 113, pp. 378–79 (2).

54. See TB, no. 113, p. 379 (3).

On Human Life,
Humanae Vitae

General Audience Addresses 114 to 129

A. INTRODUCTION

The fifth cycle of theology of the body discussed the question of marriage as presented primarily in the fifth chapter of Ephesians. As we have seen, in that analysis of marriage John Paul applied the results of the study of the human person in the body/person structure that was undertaken in the first three cycles. In those cycles, as the reader may remember, the pope discussed the human person in the garden of Eden before sin (first cycle); after sin, that is, historical man (second cycle); and after the second coming and the final resurrection (third cycle). These three cycles took their points of origin from the words of Christ that divorce was not allowed "in the beginning" (first cycle), that looking lustfully constitutes "adultery in the heart" (second cycle), and that after the final resurrection there is no giving and taking in marriage (third cycle). In each of these three conditions of the human person, the human body manifests, reveals, and expresses the human person, but in different ways. The results of these analyses illuminated the question of virginity and celibacy in the fourth cycle and the question of marriage in the fifth cycle.

In the final cycle of the theology of the body (addresses 114 to 129), which is the crowning conclusion of the entire set of reflections, John Paul rereads the encyclical of Pope Paul VI, *Humanae Vitae* (On Human Life), promulgated on July 25, 1968. The rereading of the famous "birth control" encyclical is undertaken in light of the results of the first three cycles and of the fifth cycle.

In *Humanae Vitae* Pope Paul VI responded to the advent of the contraceptive pill in the early 1960s by authoritatively teaching that the pill and all other contraceptive devices were immoral violations of the marital union of husband and wife. It is fair to say that no teaching of the church since the sixteenth century has been as thoroughly ignored and even rejected as Pope Paul VI's *Humanae Vitae*. In fact, it was rejected before it was even read!

1. The Rejection of the Encyclical

On the evening July 25, 1968, the day the encyclical was released in Rome but before the text of the pope's new document was available in the United States (those were the days before the instant electronic movement of documents via the Internet), interested parties on the East Coast of the United States were calling prominent scholars, theologians, priests, and religious brothers and sisters to solicit their names for a full-page ad to appear the next day in the *New York Times,* opposing the teaching of Pope Paul VI. While some refused to lend their names to the ad, partly because they believed it was patently unfair to oppose something from the pope that they had not even read, sixty-seven Catholic priests, scholars, and religious signed this ad. *Humanae Vitae* might be said to have been dead on arrival, at least in the United States.

Catholics in other parts of the world reacted with as much or more opposition. At least two national conferences of bishops voiced unprecedented objections to the papal teaching.[1] Although Pope Paul VI must have known that his teaching would raise a bit of a storm, he was probably stunned at the violence of the opposition. It is interesting to note that from July 1968 until his death in August 1978, Pope Paul VI never issued another encyclical. Some suggest that the reason was the opposition that *Humanae Vitae* occasioned.

2. Why the Theology of the Body: Address 129

John Paul alludes to the storm over *Humanae Vitae* when he writes in address 129, the last address of the theology of the body series, that "in responding to some questions of today in the field of conjugal and family morality, at the same time the encyclical also raised other questions, as we know, of a biomedical nature. But also (and above all) they are of a theological nature: they belong to that sphere of anthropology and theology that we have called the theology of the body. The reflections we made consist in facing the questions raised with regard to the encyclical *Humanae Vitae.* The reaction that the encyclical aroused confirms the importance and the difficulty of these questions."[2] The pope goes on to write that the questions arising from *Humanae Vitae* "permeate the sum total of our reflections."[3] In other words, John Paul determined very early in his pontificate, within the first year, to address the questions arising from *Humanae Vitae* through his theology of the body.

3. Objective and Subjective Points of View

The pope specifically notes that the theology of the body constitutes a development of divine revelation, because it examines the "problem" of *Humanae Vitae* from the point of view of the individual human person. "The analysis of the personalistic aspects of the Church's doctrine, contained in Pope Paul VI's encyclical, emphasizes a determined appeal to measure man's progress on the basis of the person, that is, of what is good for man as man—what corresponds to his essential dignity. The analysis of the personalistic aspects leads to the conviction that the encyclical presents as a fundamental problem the viewpoint of man's authentic development. This development is measured to the greatest extent on the basis of ethics and not only on technology."[4]

In the teaching of Pope Paul VI in *Humanae Vitae*, John Paul recognizes a profound truth about human persons taught in an *objective* way. As always, John Paul wants to show that the objective truth of the church's teaching is also, from the individual, *subjective* viewpoint, the only path to follow for authentic personal development. Not only does John Paul accept that God created each of us in such a way as to exclude what Paul VI excludes in *Humanae Vitae*, he demonstrates through the theology of the body that the individual who acts contrary to the teaching in *Humanae Vitae* harms himself or herself and acts contrary to his or her best interests.

One of the key points is that the sins of contraception, sterilization, and abortion examined in *Humanae Vitae* are sins not just because "God said so," but because they involve a manipulation and use of human persons. Since persons are to be loved, not used, such sins damage, harm, and hurt the individual who engages in these sins and all those who participate in these sins. The sins listed in *Humanae Vitae* are sins not just because they violate the biological laws of the human body established by God when he created us, but because they are attacks against the human body, that is, attacks against human persons. As we quoted above, *Humanae Vitae* raised questions of "a bio-medical nature." But these "belong to that sphere of anthropology and theology that we have called theology of the body," because the human body is not just a collection of biological functions but the expression of the individual human person. When one touches the body, one touches the person!

Therefore, as the pope writes, his reflection on *Humanae Vitae* in the sixth cycle of the theology of the body "is not artificially added to the sum total but is organically and homogeneously united with it."[5] In rereading *Humanae Vitae* in this sixth cycle, the pope makes use of the conclusions from the first three cycles and from the fifth cycle. It is obvious, then, that it is necessary to summarize the conclusions from the first three cycles and the fifth before we begin to explore what John Paul is teaching in this final cycle of the theology of the body.

The burden of the first and second cycles of the theology of the body is to establish that the human body is the expression of the human person. Further, since each human person is an image of God, not only are we called to express our own persons in and through our bodies, but through our very humanity, our creation in the image and likeness of God, we are called to act as God acts and express those acts in and through our human bodies. The human body then can be said to speak a language, the language of our persons, and even the language of God. In and through our flesh and blood, when we act as God acts, we, individually, reveal something of our own persons and something of God. Since God loves, we are called to love as he loves and express those loving acts in and through our bodies. The human body, in its masculinity and femininity, reveals to us that we are called to love, to make a self-donation of ourselves to others. This is the nuptial meaning of the body. Adam and Eve made such a self-donation to each other and lived a loving communion in the garden of Eden before sin.

However, sin entered human history when Adam and Eve yielded to the temptations of Satan. This fall caused a rupture within man, so that the human body no longer always and infallibly responded to the dictates of the personal powers in man, that is, to the mind and the will. There was a "constitutive break within the human person, . . . almost a rupture of man's original spiritual and somatic unity."[6] It became very difficult for human persons to love as they should. This condition was revealed to Adam and Eve in and through their bodies by their changed experience of their own nakedness after sin. Still, they were not completely destroyed, and they were still called to love as before and to express that love in and through their bodies. Now, however, they needed the help of a redeemer, so God the Son became man, suffered, died, was buried, and rose from the dead, accomplishing the redemption of the body. This redemption of the body means that human persons now have the help of divine grace, which makes it possible, if not easy, to love as we should. But that love requires an effort, even with the help of grace. That effort is the work of purity, of the power to see in everyone, most especially in those of the opposite sex, the dignity and value of the person revealed in and through their masculinity or femininity.

The first and second cycles showed that there were two ways the human body speaks the language of personhood: in the garden of Eden before sin and in historical man after sin, redeemed by Christ. There is a third way: the fulfillment of the redemption of the body. That third way will be realized after the second coming, when our bodies will be resurrected and reunited with our souls. This third way that the body speaks the language of personhood was sketched in the third cycle of the theology of the body.

The fifth cycle of the theology of the body series concluded that the sacrament of creation, that is, God's visibility in and through a human body, was taken up again in Christ, who made God perfectly visible, because his body expressed and revealed God the Father, Son, and Holy Spirit. Adam and Eve's human bodies spoke the language of personhood; that is, they revealed themselves in and through their bodies, but they also revealed God himself. Further, the first couple were graced in their love for one another. Theirs was a spousal love that revealed the mystery hidden in God from all eternity. The spousal character of Christ's love is grounded, primarily, on the foundation of making the mystery hidden in God from all eternity visible in and through a human body, and secondarily, on the gracing that Christ accomplished as compared with the gracing of our first parents. Therefore, the sacrament of redemption is founded on the sacrament of creation. But all this can be accomplished only if the human body, in speaking the language of personhood, speaks that language truthfully.

B. Married Couples Reread the Language of the Body in Truth: Addresses 114 to 116

In the first address of the sixth cycle (114), John Paul notes that he does not plan to comment on the entire text of *Humanae Vitae* but only on the central passage, which speaks of the two significances of the marital act: conjugal love and procreation. In the theology of the body, John Paul usually uses the term "significances" of the marital act. In the usual English translation of *Humanae Vitae*, the Latin for "significances" is translated as "meanings." Thus *Humanae Vitae* speaks of the two "meanings" of the marital act; that is, the conjugal meaning and the procreative meaning. Since we are following the theology of the body addresses, we will use the English translation found in theology of the body. As is well known, Pope Paul VI taught that there was an inseparable connection between these two significances of the marital act and that they cannot be separated if the couple is not to sin. A married couple should never engage in the conjugal act without authentic love that includes an openness to the procreation of children.

1. The Thesis of the Sixth Cycle

The pope remarks that in the physical union of husband and wife during the conjugal act, it is especially important that the "language of the body be reread in truth. This reading becomes the indispensable condition for acting in truth, that is, for behaving in accordance with the value and the moral norm."[7] The couple, each in his or her own way, must reread the language of each of their bodies in the midst of the conjugal act and realize the truth, the value, expressed. If they do their rereading properly, the couple will *subjectively* internalize the *objective* teaching of the encyclical. They will not be in a state of tension regarding the two significances. The two significances will become one reality for them, under the rubric of their loving union.

The norm that the two significances of the marital act are inseparable "determines the morality of the acts of the man and the woman in the marriage act." John Paul points out that "the encyclical leads one to seek the foundation for the norm . . . in the nature of this very act, and more deeply still, in the nature of the subjects themselves who are performing the act."[8] This line is the central thesis of the last cycle. The norm of Paul VI's encyclical is revealed to the husband and wife in the midst of the conjugal union through their rereading of the language of their bodies. The norm is known through the spouses' own experience of the conjugal union, during which they come to know the language that each of their bodies speaks. The teaching of the encyclical is not "out there" in the sense that it is an objective norm *imposed* on the couple. Rather, it is found in the language of their own bodies.

John Paul finds that *Humanae Vitae* points to this truth; that is, that the inseparable connection of the two significances of the marital act can be known by the couple if they correctly read the language of their own bodies. Paul VI writes that the two significances of the marital act are found in the "fundamental structure" of the marital act written into the very nature of man and woman. The two significances are found in the act itself, that is, as John Paul interprets it, in the two subjects, the husband and wife themselves, and precisely in their bodies. So, "the fundamental structure (that is, the nature) of the marriage act constitutes the necessary basis for an adequate reading and discovery of the two significances that must be carried over into the conscience and the decisions of the acting parties."[9] The couple must come to an awareness through the language of the body of the meaning of the marital act and realize themselves that the two significances are inseparable. This realization will then become part of their consciousness and will shape their consciences. As always, John Paul II shows that the ethical norms of the gospel must become part of the subject, of the person, who then acts in accordance with those norms.

John Paul's argument, in part, is that the truth of the moral norms can be experienced and read in the lives of individuals if they act in accordance with the truth. In the case of norms pertaining to bodily acts—which means in the case of most of the moral norms—they are experienced and revealed in and through those very bodily acts. The perception of the norms by the individual or individuals depends on their reading the language of the body according to truth, that is, reading it as it is given, without any false preconceived notions.

In the next address (115) John Paul reviews the fact that the norm taught in *Humanae Vitae* is contained in the natural law and belongs to the content of the church's tradition. The teaching of the encyclical "is in accordance with the sum total of revealed doctrine contained in biblical sources (cf. *HV* 4)."[10] However, and more important for the purposes of John Paul's commentary, the norm of *Humanae Vitae* can be found by couples rereading the language of their bodies in truth.

2. The Teaching Against Contraception Is Truly Pastoral

In address 116 John Paul links *Humanae Vitae* with *Gaudium et Spes* (The Pastoral Constitution on the Church in the Modern World). Both documents are pastoral in the sense that they respond to practical questions raised by the men and women of the contemporary world. Further, both documents were inspired by a genuine concern for the authentic good of each and every person in the world. "Whoever believes that the Council and the encyclical do not sufficiently take into account the difficulties present in concrete life does not understand the pastoral concern that was at the origin of those documents. Pastoral concern means the search for the true good of man, a promotion of the values engraved in his person by God."[11] Further, it is impossible that "the values engraved" in the human person by God cannot be lived. The same God who "engraved" those values created the universe in which human persons live, and God cannot contradict himself. Therefore, if these values can be correctly read in the individual lives of every human person, they can also be fulfilled.

However, it is not just married couples who object to Paul VI's teaching, it is also society. Modern society presents the argument that the norm of *Humanae Vitae* is not possible because the good of marriage requires the conjugal embrace, but the good of society—as well as the good of the couple—requires a certain control over population. Thus the two inseparable significances of the marital act, as taught in *Humanae Vitae,* seem to be in conflict. Few would doubt the necessity of an authentic loving conjugal embrace in marriage, but many doubt the necessity of every one of these marital acts being "open to the transmission of life." It is argued that truly responsible couples engage in the marital act frequently for the good of their marriage, but at the same time, should limit the size of their families. Therefore, responsible parenthood requires the modern couple to separate the two significances of the marital act. In facing this argument, the pope turns in the next five addresses (117 to 121) to the question of responsible parenthood.

C. RESPONSIBLE PARENTHOOD: ADDRESSES 117 TO 121

If the two significances of the marital act are to be maintained in accordance with its fundamental structure, spouses must exercise a certain prudence and judgment especially in regard to procreation. In address 117, we find several quotations regarding this point from the Pastoral Constitution on the Church in the Modern World. Conjugal love and the responsible transmission of life must be harmonized. In considering whether to try to conceive or to avoid the conception of a child, spouses should "thoughtfully take into account both their own welfare and that of their children, those already born and those which the future may bring," as well as the times, society, and their own state in life. However, "it is the married couple themselves who must in the last analysis arrive at these judgments before God."[12]

"All this is possible only if the virtue of married chastity is seriously practiced (*Gaudium et Spes,* section 51)."[13] Of course, responsible parenthood is not simply the case of a couple postponing a pregnancy, but it can mean that couples will try to conceive. For some couples, responsible parenthood could mean a large family, and for others it could mean a small family. The task of each couple is to discern whether it is prudent to try to postpone a pregnancy or try to conceive a new human person.

1. It Is Possible to Express a Lie with the Body

In address 118 John Paul reminds couples that even if they have sufficient prudential reasons to avoid a pregnancy, it is important for them to do so by the right means. Even if a couple is motivated by "acceptable reasons" to avoid a pregnancy, the use of contraception is still immoral, because spouses should never change the "very structure of the conjugal act."[14]

The following address (119), rests on almost everything already laid down in the theology of the body. The pope reminds us that the language of the body expressed in the conjugal union is a complete self-gift of each spouse to the other. The bodies of the husband and the wife express and reveal their persons. In their wedding vows, they chose to give themselves to each other in the union of marriage. This gift is expressed, renewed, and made concrete in the marital act. They speak their total gift of themselves to each other in the language of their bodies during the marital act. The marital act is not a true self-gift made by each of them to the other if they do not give themselves completely in their entire being, in all the potentialities of their persons, body and soul. If in the midst of the gift, they should hold back, refuse to give, some aspect of their selves, then the language of their bodies that expresses a self-gift, is in fact a lie.

As the pope taught in *Familiaris Consortio* (Apostolic Exhortation on the Family), "The innate language that expresses the total reciprocal self-giving of husband and wife is overlaid, through contraception, by an objectively contradictory language, namely, that of not giving oneself totally to the other. This leads not only to a positive refusal to be open to life but also to a falsification of the inner truth of conjugal love, which is called upon to give itself in personal totality."[15] The contraceptive marital act is not an act of love, because the conjugal union is "deprived of its interior truth."[16]

The act's interior truth—the truth of the spouses' bodies—includes the possibility of new life. In effect, the couple contracepting speaks a lie with the language of their bodies.

2. The Marital Embrace as Gift

A gift is a disinterested present made by one person to another to benefit the recipient, not the giver. For example, at Christmas time, we try to give gifts that will please and benefit those who receive them. If, in giving, we try to benefit ourselves—for instance, if a brother gives his sister a new CD player only because he wants to use it all the time—this is quickly recognized as a non-gift, as an act that benefits the supposed giver and not the recipient.

The marital act is a gift of one spouse to the other for the sake of the other. Clearly, then, the act must not be done for the benefit of the one giving. Of course, since both have this attitude and the act is a mutual giving, both usually benefit; but the motive of each must be for the benefit of the other. Selfishness is excluded from the marital act.

3. Self-Mastery or Manipulation

Obviously, given the "constitutive break within the human person,"[17] it is difficult in the sexual union to make a disinterested gift to one's spouse. Such an act requires self-mastery. The problem with contraception is that instead of a self-mastery, that is, a postponement of the marital act for the sake of responsible parenthood, the couple claims a control over their own bodies. They "manipulate and degrade"[18] themselves so that they may engage in the marital act without the possibility of new life. In *Humanae Vitae* Paul VI compared the "domination . . . of the forces of nature" with "mastery of self."[19] Regarding these two forms of control, John Paul remarks that "the problem consists in maintaining an adequate relationship between what is defined as 'domination . . . of the forces of nature' (*HV* 2), and the 'mastery of self' (*HV* 21) which is indispensable for the human person. Modern man shows a tendency to transfer the methods proper to the former to those of the latter. 'Man has made stupendous progress in the domination and rational organization of the forces of nature,' we read in the encyclical, 'to the point that he is endeavoring to extend this control over every aspect of his own life—over his body, over his mind and emotions, over his social life, and even over the laws that regulate the transmission of life' (*HV* 2). This extension of the sphere of the means of 'domination of the forces of nature' menaces the human person for whom the method of 'self-mastery' is and remains specific. . . . The resort to artificial means destroys the constitutive dimension of the person. It deprives man of the subjectivity proper to him and makes him an object of manipulation."[20]

Technology is very good, but it must be applied to the human person according to the structure of the person, body and soul. The human body speaks the language of personhood through all of its major functions, so none of these healthy, major functions should ever be altered, harmed, or destroyed. To do so is to attack the body as the expression of the person; it is to manipulate the person as an object, a thing. Contraception does attack our personhood in precisely this way. It alters and harms our healthy fertility, a major bodily function.

4. Natural Methods versus Contraception

In address 120 John Paul teaches that there is a radical difference between a couple who avoid conception by engaging in the marital act only at infertile times and a couple who contracept. He further teaches that "in the case of a morally upright regulation of fertility effected by means of periodic continence, one is clearly dealing with the practice of conjugal chastity, that is, of a definite ethical attitude. In biblical language we could say that it is a case of living by the Spirit (cf. Gal 5:25)."[21]

In address 121 one of the themes of the sixth cycle is stressed again: "The concept of a morally correct regulation of fertility is nothing other than the rereading of the language of the body in truth. . . . It is necessary to bear in mind that the body speaks not merely with the whole external expression of masculinity and femininity, but also with the internal structures of the organism."[22]

One of the criticisms of Pope Paul VI's teaching in *Humanae Vitae* was that it rested moral truths on human biology. The question was asked, "If we can dam up rivers, defy gravity by flying, launch men and machines so that they can journey to the moon, why cannot we alter our own biology? Why is human biology off-limits, but gravity is not?" John Paul answers that the body is more than its biological parts. Through these apparently understandable functions, the mystery of the human person, and even the mystery of God, is expressed.

One way of thinking about this is the old line of high school biology teachers that the human body is worth less than $10 in terms of the chemicals it has within it. Would anyone actually take $10 for a child's life? Of course not. We are more than the sum of our biological parts. In and through the body, the mystery of personhood is expressed. We dare not reduce a human person to his or her biology. But if couples are to exercise responsible parenthood and at the same time speak the language of self-gift in and through their bodies, it is obviously necessary that they develop a self-mastery, or what is sometimes called continence.

D. Continence and Self-mastery with the Help of Grace: Addresses 122 to 127[23]

There is no question that marriage is a daunting task assigned to married couples. But they have help. We are reminded in address 122 that the power of the Holy Spirit is poured into their hearts through the sacraments, especially the Eucharist and reconciliation. "These are the means—infallible and indispensable—for forming the Christian spirituality of married life and family life. With these, that essential and spiritual creative power of love reaches human hearts and, at the same time, human bodies in their subjective masculinity and femininity."[24]

John Paul's confidence in the power of the Holy Spirit is accompanied with realism about the difficulty couples may encounter in their growth in continence. He quotes Paul VI's statement in *Humanae Vitae*, "We have no wish at all to pass over in silence the difficulties, at times very great, which beset the lives of Christian married couples." John Paul remarks that in the encyclical, "the view of married life is marked at every step by Christian realism."[25]

In the next address (123), John Paul speaks about the opposition that we face in the process of developing continence. "The powers of concupiscence try to detach the language of the body from the truth, that is, they try to falsify it," he observes. Nevertheless, "the power of love instead strengthens it ever anew in that truth, so that the mystery of the redemption of the body can bear fruit in it."[26] In this passage, John Paul asserts that the power of love safeguards the language of the body in the marital embrace. It is important to remember that the language of the body in the marital embrace, as he has previously mentioned, includes the possibility of procreation. Therefore, love has the role of "safeguarding the inseparable connection between the 'two meanings' of the conjugal act."[27]

Love unites the two meanings into one reality because love is the self-gift of the spouses, their whole beings, to each other. They could not love, they could not give themselves completely to each other and reciprocally accept the gift of the other without at the same time giving and accepting that part of themselves that includes the possibility of life. Another way of looking at the same problem is to realize that love is *the* activity of God, spectacularly manifested in the life of Christ, particularly in his passion, death, and resurrection. His love was a union of wills ("Not my will but yours be done"), founded on the knowledge that the dignity and value implanted in each and every human being required for its fulfillment that there be at least a possibility of heaven for each and every individual. Love in Christ, then, is a union of wills based on the recognition of the value of dignity of the one loved. Christ's love was a self-gift (what more could he have given that what he gave on the cross?). Christ's love is also permanent and life giving. He remained on the cross to the bitter end, and he retains the wounds of his passion in his humanity even now in heaven and will be marked by those wounds for all eternity. From his wounded side flowed blood and water, the source of the sacramental life of the church. Love then has five characteristics: (1) a union of wills created through a choice that is (2) founded on the dignity of the person loving and the dignity of the one or ones loved and is (3) a self-gift, (4) permanent, and (5) life-giving. Authentic love unites the two meanings of the marital act into one reality. There really are not two things, but one: love. But

love cannot be given or received without self-mastery, without overcom-
the falsification of love caused by concupiscence. For this reason, couples
ently require the love poured out to them by the Holy Spirit through the
raments, especially those of the Eucharist and reconciliation.

1. Self-Mastery Is Essential for Love

Love is founded on the recognition of the dignity and value of oneself
and of the one loved. The recognition of the dignity of the other is the
reason why one would choose to make the stupendous gift of oneself.
Self-mastery, or continence, is required for the recognition of the dignity
of the other because, as we read in address 124, "concupiscence of the
flesh itself, insofar as it seeks above all carnal and sensual satisfaction,
makes man in a certain sense blind and insensitive to the most profound
values."[28] If all a husband considers when he sees his wife is "what can
she do for me," that is, if he is looking at her solely as one that can satisfy
his desires, he does not see her as a person created for her own sake. He
does not see the awesome and fearful dignity and value with which God
created her. Rather, he sees her as a thing, something to be used. This is a
reduction of the incredible dignity of a human person to an object. Such
a reduction prevents love, because love depends on the recognition of the
dignity and value both of the one loved and the loving.

Concupiscence is the inordinate desire for sexual gratification. If one
or both spouses act out of concupiscence, they reduce each other's significance to only one value: his or her ability to satisfy a sexual desire. In this
reduction, the other person is not seen as he or she is, but only according
to one aspect. As concupiscence is indulged, it grows, and the blindness
to the full reality of the other person becomes deeper. Finally, the other is
seen solely as the one who satisfies the sexual desire. Eventually, others
will be found who will do this in a new or more exciting way. Blindness
to the full truth of the other person makes the love-union of marriage
impossible. Even if the marriage does not end in divorce, there remains
little of the original communion of persons that the spouses supposedly
commenced when they said their vows. Since we are created as images of

God to love as he loves, a loveless marriage renders life empty, because "life is senseless" without love.[29]

By contrast, John Paul observes, self-mastery will cause couples to "defer to one another out of reverence for Christ" (Ephesians 5:21). This biblical injunction "seems to open that interior space in which both become ever more sensitive to the most profound and most mature values that are connected with the spousal significance of the body and with the true freedom of the gift. Conjugal chastity (and chastity in general) is manifested at first as the capacity to resist the concupiscence of the flesh. It later gradually reveals itself as a singular capacity to perceive, love and practice those meanings of the language of the body which remain altogether unknown to concupiscence itself. Those meanings progressively enrich the marital dialogue of the couple, purifying it, deepening it, and at the same time simplifying it."[30]

Self-mastery, achieved through continence, allows one to look beyond the spouse solely as one who merely satisfies sexual longing—the sexual desire to possess the other person in order to satisfy oneself. In mastering this longing, one does not give up any hope of receiving the other, although it may *seem* like that on occasion, especially at first. Rather the sexual longing is subordinated, so that one will be able to receive the other as a true gift in all the mystery and awe of his or her personhood. When this occurs, spouses marvel at the absolutely astonishing gift they have received: another human person, in his or her entire mystery. Each wonders, "How can I be so incredibly fortunate as to be the recipient of the self-gift of this other marvelous, wondrous person?" The joy of receiving this gift so transcends any merely carnal satisfaction that no one would ever want to return to merely seeking sexual satisfaction from the other. Further, the awe and wonder at the gift of the spouse extends to an awe and wonder at the creative power of God who created the spouse and enabled him or her to give himself or herself. The awe and wonder at the gift of the spouse and at God turns to gratitude, and gratitude increases love. In such couples, love of each other and of God grows daily.

2. Self-Mastery and Responsible Parenthood

Love solves the contradiction that some people have claimed to find in *Humanae Vitae*. It has been argued that if it is not appropriate for a particular couple to conceive a child but contraception is not allowed, the spouses would be deprived of their marital right to the conjugal union. However, there is no contradiction in Paul VI's teaching. If each spouse accepts the other as an infinitely valuable person, and this includes accepting the spouse's fertility, both will refuse to harm the other or the marriage. If it is not prudent to bring a child into the world, and if both spouses truly love the other, neither will insist on the privilege of marriage at the fertile time. Such insistence would not be an act of love but simply a surrender to sexual longing. Such a surrender is excluded by the love each has for the other. The sexual longing is subordinated to the love and is mastered through continence for the sake of the much greater gift. As the pope writes in address 124, "It is indeed a matter of not doing harm to the communion of the couple in the case where for just reasons they should abstain from the conjugal act."[31]

Neither Pope Paul VI nor Pope John Paul II is teaching that this is easy for couples, especially at first. They do, however, insist that this is the only path to true happiness, because the only "way" for man is love—to paraphrase some language John Paul II used in his first encyclical, *Redemptor Hominis*.[32] As John Paul notes in the next address (125), "It is often thought that continence causes inner tensions which man must free himself from. In the light of the analyses we have done, continence, understood integrally, is rather the only way to free man from such tensions."[33]

3. Human Beings Should Not Be Driven by Emotion and Sensuality

When a man and a woman are coming to know each other, they experience sensual reactions and emotional excitement. The sensual reactions might be regarded as the anticipation of the pleasure of the conjugal act. The emotional response, conditioned by the masculinity or femininity of the other, is often expressed by "manifestations of affection."[34]

Continence does not suppress these reactions but directs them according to the true value of the other person. "Continence is not only . . . the ability to abstain," John Paul writes. "It is the ability to direct the respective reactions, both as to their content and their character."[35]

Following this line of thought, the pope teaches in address 126 that "the knowledge itself of the rhythms of fertility—even though indispensable—still does not create that interior freedom of the gift, which is by its nature explicitly spiritual and depends on man's interior maturity. This freedom presupposes such a capacity to direct the sensual and emotive reactions as to make possible the giving of self to the other 'I' on the grounds of the mature self-possession of one's own 'I' in its corporeal and emotive subjectivity."[36] In other words, if I have self-mastery, I possess myself in the proper sense and can make a gift of myself. Without such self-mastery, there can be no authentic love.

It is also true that couples grow in continence and self-mastery as they "defer to one another out of reverence for Christ." By practicing chastity and continence, couples become more and more chaste. They are able to achieve self-mastery.

4. Natural Family Planning

One of the tools couples may use to grow in continence and chastity is the practice of Natural Family Planning (NFP). NFP is best defined as the knowledge of a couple's fertility. The practice of NFP is defined as responsible parenthood. Couples learn to identify the signs of their mutual fertility and apply that knowledge either to trying to conceive a child or to postpone conception. By refraining from the marital embrace at the appropriate times, either because the couple wishes to achieve a pregnancy or because they wish to postpone one, they grow in self-mastery and continence. This effort, in turn, develops in them an authentic love for each other and for God.

Almost every bishop, priest, and deacon has had the experience of witnessing the marriage of a young couple who have begun their marriage with a relatively ungenerous attitude toward future children but have agreed to take a course in NFP. The couple may want to use a natural method rather than a chemical or barrier method of spacing their children. They faithfully apply the knowledge of their fertility and attempt to exercise responsible parenthood, abstaining from the marital embrace at the times they believe it imprudent to conceive a child. Then, experiencing some difficulty in achieving a pregnancy, they abstain a bit, in order to maximize the chance of conceiving a child. The first child is born, and husband and wife, now mother and father, see the wondrous, awesome gift God has given to them in the child. They see their own humanity reproduced. They come to know each other in a different way, as mother and father, and their appreciation of each other and gratitude to each other grow immensely. They each come to see the mystery of their spouse more and more clearly, and each is awed at the gift he or she has received from each other, that is, the child. Their love for each other grows, as does their love for their baby. They also see in the child a reflection of the divine. They realize that they are not solely responsible for the creation of this child, but that God has had a part in it.

Their gratitude at the awesome gift of their child grows into a greater and greater love for God. Love is of itself generous; it wishes to share itself with others. As the spouses grow in their love for each other, their child, and God, they become more and more generous. Some years later, they visit the parish where the bishop, priest, or deacon who witnessed their marriage is serving. They now have—let's say, by way of example—four children. The pastor remembers them and also remembers that while they agreed to use NFP, they said that they were going to limit the size of their family to two children. He sees them with four and asks why they changed their minds. They cannot explain what happened. But what happened, even if they do not fully realize it, is that their love for each other, for their children, and for God grew and grew. The practice of NFP was a school of love for that family. Of course, this example is not intended to diminish or to denigrate in any way the challenges of family life today. But, without love, those challenges can seem impossible. With love they are manageable.

For the church, the pope hints, the practice of NFP is only secondarily a means of spacing children, although it certainly is that; it is primarily a school of love. Obviously, as the pope has said repeatedly, the practice of NFP can become a school of love only if it is accompanied with prayer and frequent reception of the sacraments.

5. The Gifts of the Holy Spirit

In address 127 John Paul stresses the importance of the gifts of the Holy Spirit for spouses' efforts to develop the proper attitude of love toward one another. In speaking about the sacraments and prayer, the pope previously accented sanctifying grace, the life of God we receive through the sacraments. In this address and the next one (128), he mentions the more transcendent work of the Holy Spirit through the seven gifts.

Couples need to develop a reverential fear before one another as belonging to the Lord. This fear of the Lord does not mean that husband and wife cower in terror, but that they have an awe at the work of God in creating the other spouse—and in creating their children. Each of us reflects God in our own unique ways. Each of us is an icon, an image, of God. In recognizing the divine mystery present in each other, spouses need to see in one another the spark of the divine. Respect for each other "is manifested also as a salvific fear. It is a fear of violating or degrading what bears in itself the sign of the divine mystery of creation."[37] As the gift matures, this fear amounts to a "veneration for the essential values of the conjugal union . . . veneration for the interior truth of the mutual language of the body."[38]

The gift of the Holy Spirit that is called the fear of the Lord helps us to hold in awe everything that is sacred and holy. Every single human person is, in a sense, sacred and holy. Since spouses touch the mystery of each other in an extraordinarily profound way—more profoundly than occurs in any other human relationship—their awe and wonder, their "salvific fear," is of vital importance. The gift of salvific fear in the presence of the sacred can help spouses to hold each other always in great awe and wonder and remind them of the gift that each of them is to the other.

Continuing the same theme in address 128, John Paul writes, "The attitude of respect for the work of God, which the Spirit stirs up in the couple, has an enormous significance," because it develops in the couple a "capacity for deep satisfaction, admiration, disinterested attention to the visible and at the same time the invisible beauty of femininity and masculinity, and finally a deep appreciation for the disinterested gift of the other."[39]

The argument of Pope John Paul II for the teaching of *Humanae Vitae* in the sixth cycle of theology of the body can be summarized as follows. Authentic love is not possible without self-mastery, which only is attained with an effort of the will aided by the virtue of continence given through God's grace. Therefore, the sacraments are essential to authentic love. In addition, the gifts of the Holy Spirit help the couple develop that awe and wonder at each other that helps them to "reverence each other"[40] as they would Christ. Authentic love always includes the possibility of life, because without such a possibility, there is no love.

We quoted from the last address (129) in the beginning of our discussion of the sixth cycle of theology of the body, so it will not be necessary to summarize it here.

E. CONCLUSION

There is no question that the entire corpus of Pope John Paul II's theology of the body was intended as an exposition of the teaching of *Humanae Vitae*. However, it is much more than that. Taking Christ's words as the departure point, the first three cycles of theology of the body represent a theological experiment using the data of the earliest human experiences recorded in Genesis as a mine of material for a phenomenological examination of the human person. But since these recorded experiences are contained in the inspired word of God, the language used to record them also contains revelation about ourselves and God. The phenomenological examination of human experiences leads to questions about the meaning of human life—as well as some incomplete answers. But the revelation of the Scriptures answers such questions definitively. The combination of phenomenology (data about the human person) and revelation (answers to the questions about the human person) yields a double flow of data about the human person and a new way of formulating the truths contained in revelation. Therefore, the first three cycles of theology of the body result in a genuine development in our understanding of the mystery of human personhood as revealed to us by God most definitively in Christ.

The fifth cycle reformulates the teaching of St. Paul in Ephesians 5 on marriage and its sacramentality in light of the previous analyses in the first three cycles. This reformulation yields new insights and new developments. The fourth cycle on celibacy and virginity might seem out of place at first, but is vitally necessary as a prelude to the discussion of the sacramentality of marriage, because celibacy and virginity are for the sake of the kingdom of heaven, and that is the goal also of the sacrament of marriage, for spouses are to help each other come to the glory of heaven. In this fourth cycle, as in the fifth, there are some new developments. Indeed, while each cycle in its own way prepares for the crowning conclusion found in the sixth cycle, each cycle also contains new insights and new ways of teaching what the gospel has always taught. Needless to say, the rereading of *Humanae Vitae* in the sixth cycle is not just a rereading but a genuine deepening, or grounding, of the teaching of that encyclical in the roots of the theology of the body.

We must all always and everywhere give thanks to God for the teaching of Pope John Paul II in the theology of the body—and for everything else he taught the world in his twenty-six years as the Vicar of Christ!

1. The conferences were the Canadian and the Austrian.
2. See TB, address 129, pp. 420–21 (2).
3. See TB, address 129, p. 422 (4).
4. See TB, address 129, pp. 421–22 (3).
5. See TB, address 129, p. 422 (4).
6. See TB, address 28, p. 115 (2).
7. See TB, address 114, p. 387 (4).
8. See TB, address 114, p. 387 (5).
9. See TB, address 114, p. 387 (6).
10. See TB, address 115, p. 389 (3).
11. See TB, address 116, p. 392 (6).

12. See TB, address 117, p. 393 (2).

13. See TB, address 117, p. 393 (1).

14. See TB, address 118, p. 395 (2).

15. See *Familiaris Consortio,* 32.

16. See TB, address 119, p. 398 (6).

17. See TB, address 28, p. 115 (2). See also above, Cycle 2, pp. 77–78.

18. See *Familiaris Consortio,* 32.

19. See *Humanae Vitae,* 2 and 21.

20. See TB, address 119, pp. 396–97 (1).

21. See TB, address 120, p. 401 (6). See also above, Cycle 5, pp. 178–80.

22. See TB, address 121, p. 402 (1).

23. See above, Cycle 2, pp. 100–6, addresses 50–53. In addresses 122–127 some of the ideas of addresses 50–53 are repeated. However, in addresses 50–53 John Paul's viewpoint is grace leading to continence and self-mastery, enabling the individual human person to overcome the constitutive break within himself/herself. In addresses 12–127, the pope's viewpoint is grace leading to continence/self-mastery, enabling couples to live a marriage properly. Further, addresses 50–53 use "purity," whereas "continence" is used in the sixth cycle. "Purity pertains more to the individual, and "continence," to the relationship in marriage.

24. See TB, address 122, p. 406 (5).

25. See TB, address 122, p. 405 (4).

26. See TB, address 123, p. 406 (1).

27. See TB, address 123, p. 406 (2).

28. See TB, address 124, p. 409 (2).

29. See *Redemptor Hominis,* 10. The full quotation is: "Man cannot live without love. He remains a being that is incomprehensible for himself, his life is senseless."

30. See TB, address 124, p. 409 (3).

31. See TB, address 124, p. 410 (6).

32. See *Redemptor Hominis,* 10, 13.

33. See TB, address 125, p. 411 (1).

34. See TB, address 125, p. 413 (6).

35. See TB, address 125, p. 412 (5). The reference here to excitement and sensual reactions hearkens back to what the pope wrote in *Love and Responsibility* in the early sixties about the sensual and sensible reactions of the masculine to the feminine

and vice versa. See also Hogan and LeVoir, *Covenant of Love*, pp. 48–50.

36. See TB, address 126, p. 414 (4).

37. See TB, address 127, p. 416 (5).

38. See TB, address 127, p. 416 (5).

39. See TB, address 128, p. 417 (4).

40. See Ephesians 5:21.

Numbered List of the Theology of the Body Addresses

Since this book refers to the theology of the body addresses by number, a list is provided below that includes the corresponding title and date. Links to the complete texts of the addresses from *L'Osservatore Romano*, organized by number, title, and date, can be found at www.ewtn.com/library/PAPALDOC/ JP2TBIND.HTM. The addresses are also printed in full in Pope John Paul II, *The Theology of the Body: Human Love in the Divine Plan* (Boston: Pauline Books and Media, 1997). The titles and text vary somewhat between the two sources. The titles and page numbers given below are from *The Theology of the Body: Human Love in the Divine Plan*.

Cycle One

1. "The Unity and Indissolubility of Marriage," September 5, 1979, pp. 25–27.
2. "Analysis of the Biblical Account of Creation," September 12, 1979, pp. 27–29.
3. "The Second Account of Creation: The Subjective Definition of Man," September 19, 1979, pp. 29–32.
4. "The Boundary Between Original Innocence and Redemption," September 26, 1979, pp. 32–34.
5. "The Meaning of Man's Original Solitude," October 10, 1979, pp. 35–37.
6. "Man's Awareness of Being a Person," October 24, 1979, pp. 37–39.
7. "The Alternative between Death and Immortality Enters the Definition of Man," October 31, 1979, pp. 40–42.
8. "The Original Unity of Man and Woman," November 7, 1979, pp. 42–45, 102. (A passage inadvertently omitted from this address is printed on p. 102.)
9. "By the Communion of Persons Man Becomes the Image of God," November 14, 1979, pp. 45–48.

Cycle Two

Cycle Three

64. "Marriage and Celibacy in the Light of the Resurrection of the Body," November 11, 1981, pp. 233–35.
65. "The Living God Continually Renews the Reality of Life," November 18, 1981, pp. 235–37.
66. "The Resurrection and Theological Anthropology," December 2, 1981, pp. 238–40.
67. "The Resurrection Perfects the Person," December 9, 1981, pp. 240–43.
68. "Christ's Words on the Resurrection Complete the Revelation of the Body," December 16, 1981, pp. 243–45.
69. "The New Threshold of the Complete Truth about Man," January 13, 1982, pp. 246–49.
70. "The Doctrine of the Resurrection According to St. Paul," January 27, 1982, pp. 249–52.
71. "The Risen Body Will Be Incorruptible, Glorious, Full of Dynamism, and Spiritual," February 3, 1982, pp. 252–54.
72. "The Body's Spiritualization Will Be the Source of Its Power and Incorruptibility," February 10, 1982, pp. 255–57.

Cycle Four

73. "Virginity or Celibacy for the Sake of the Kingdom," March 10, 1982, pp. 262–64.
74. "The Vocation to Continence in This Earthly Life," March 17, 1982, pp. 264–67.
75. "Continence for the Sake of the Kingdom—and Its Spiritual Fulfillment," March 24, 1982, pp. 267–70.
76. "The Effective and Privileged Way of Continence," March 31, 1982, pp. 270–72.
77. "The 'Superiority' of Continence Does Not Devalue Marriage," April 7, 1982, pp. 273–75.
78. "Marriage and Continence Complement Each Other," April 14, 1982, pp. 276–78.

Cycle Five

96. "The Analogy of Spousal Love Indicates the Radical Character of Grace," September 29, 1982, pp. 330–33.

97. "Marriage Is the Central Point of the 'Sacrament of Creation,'" October 6, 1982, pp. 333–36.

98. "The Loss of the Original Sacrament Is Restored with Redemption in the Marriage-Sacrament," October 13, 1982, pp. 336–39.

99. "Marriage Is an Integral Part of the New Sacramental Economy," October 20, 1982, pp. 339–41.

100. "The Indissolubility of the Sacrament of Marriage in the Mystery of the Redemption of the Body," October 27, 1982, pp. 342–44.

101. "Christ Opened Marriage to the Saving Action of God," November 24, 1982, pp. 344–47.

102. "The Marriage Sacrament Is an Effective Sign of God's Saving Power," December 1, 1982, pp. 347–51.

103. "The Redemptive and Spousal Dimension of Love," December 15, 1982, pp. 351–54.

104. "The Language of the Body Is the Substratum and Content of the Sacramental Sign of Spousal Communion," January 5, 1983, pp. 354–57.

105. "The Language of the Body in the Structure of Marriage," January 12, 1983, pp. 357–60.

106. "The Sacramental Covenant in the Dimension of Sign," January 19, 1983, pp. 360–63.

107. "The Language of the Body Strengthens the Marriage Covenant," January 26, 1983, pp. 363–65.

108. "Man Is Called to Overcome Concupiscence," February 9, 1983, pp. 365–68.

109. "Reflections on the Song of Songs," May 23, 1984, pp. 368–70.

110. "Truth and Freedom—The Foundation of Love," May 30, 1984, pp. 370–72.

111. "Love Is Ever Seeking and Never Satisfied," June 6, 1984, pp. 373–75.

112. "Love Is Victorious in the Struggle between Good and Evil," June 27, 1984, pp. 375–77.

113. "The Language of the Body and the Spirituality of Marriage," July 4, 1984, pp. 378–80.

Cycle Six

114. "The Morality of the Marriage Act Is Determined by the Nature of the Act and of the Subjects," July 11, 1984, pp. 386–88.
115. "The Norm of *Humanae Vitae* Arises from the Natural Law and the Revealed Order," July 18, 1984, pp. 388–90.
116. "The Importance of Harmonizing Human Love with Respect for Life," July 25, 1984, pp. 390–92.
117. "Responsible Parenthood," August 1, 1984, pp. 393–94.
118. "Faithfulness to the Divine Plan in the Transmission of Life," August 8, 1984, pp. 395–96.
119. "The Church's Position on the Transmission of Life," August 22, 1984, pp. 396–99.
120. "A Discipline that Ennobles Human Love," August 28, 1984, pp. 399–401.
121. "Responsible Parenthood Is Linked to Moral Maturity," September 5, 1984, pp. 401–3.
122. "Prayer, Penance, and the Eucharist Are the Principal Sources of Spirituality for Married Couples," October 3, 1984, pp. 404–6.
123. "The Power of Love Is Given to Man and Woman as a Share in God's Love," October 10, 1984, pp. 406–8.
124. "Continence Protects the Dignity of the Conjugal Act," October 24, 1984, pp. 408–10.
125. "Continence Frees One from Inner Tension," October 31, 1984, pp. 411–13.
126. "Continence Deepens Personal Communion," November 7, 1984, pp. 413–15.
127. "Living According to the Spirit," November 14, 1984, pp. 415–17.
128. "Respect for the Work of God," November 21, 1984, pp. 417–19.
129. "The Redemption of the Body and the Sacramentality of Marriage," November 28, 1984, pp. 419–22.

Bibliography

Buttiglione, Rocco. *Karol Wojtyla: The Thought of the Man Who Became Pope John Paul II*. trans. Paolo Guietti and Francesca Murphy. Grand Rapids, MI: William B. Eerdmans, 1997.

Hogan, Richard M. *Dissent from the Creed*. Huntington, IN: Our Sunday Visitor, 2001.

Hogan, Richard M., and John M. LeVoir. *Covenant of Love*. 2nd ed. San Francisco: Ignatius Press, 1992.

Hogan, Richard M., and John M. LeVoir. *Faith for Today*. 2nd ed. Boston: St. Paul Books and Media, 1995.

John Paul II, *Dives in Misericordia* (On the Mercy of God). November 30, 1980.

John Paul II, *Familiaris Consortio* (Apostolic Exhortation on the Family). November 22, 1981.

John Paul II, *Laborem Exercens* (On Human Work). September 14, 1981.

John Paul II, *Redemptor Hominis* (Redeemer of Man). March 4, 1979.

John Paul II, *Salvifici Doloris* (On the Christian Meaning of Human Suffering). February 11, 1984.

John Paul II, *Veritatis Splendor* (Splendor of Truth). August 6, 1993.

Pius XII. *Mystici Corporis* (Mystical Body of Christ). June 29, 1943.

The Roman Missal: The Sacramentary. April 3, 1969. trans. International Commission on English in the Liturgy. New York: Catholic Book Publishing, 1974.

Second Vatican Council. *Gaudium et Spes* (Pastoral Constitution on the Church in the Modern World). December 7, 1965.

Weigel, George. *Witness to Hope: The Biography of Pope John Paul II*. New York: Cliff Street Books, 1999.

Wojtyla, Karol. *Love and Responsibility*, trans. H. T. Willetts. San Francisco: Ignatius Press, 1993.

Wojtyla, Karol. *Sign of Contradiction*. New York: Seabury Press, 1979.

Wojtyla, Karol. *Sources of Renewal: The Implementation of Vatican II*. trans. P. S. Falla. New York: Harper and Row, 1980.